Thermal insulation:avoiding risks

A guide to good practice building construction

Building Research Establishment   Her Majesty's Stationery Office

Price lists for all available
BRE publications can be
obtained from:
Publications Sales
Building Research Establishment
Garston, Watford, WD2 7JR
Tel (0923) 664444

The guidance in this report draws upon the research and
experience of the Building Research Establishment. It has
been subjected to public comment and amended whenever
possible to reflect a consensus of views. The report was
prepared for publication by NBA Tectonics under the
guidance of BRE staff.

This book is published jointly by
Building Research Establishment as BR143   ISBN 0 85125 383 0
and
Her Majesty's Stationery Office   ISBN 0 11 701460 5

CONTENTS

The effect of increased insulation

Research has shown that technical issues that were not important for uninsulated constructions may become more significant when they are better insulated. For example, certain parts of the construction remain colder and create a greater risk of interstitial condensation, and changes to traditional forms of construction to improve the insulation could lead to damp penetration.

It is important to anticipate these effects and, by a better understanding of the physical principles involved, avoid the risk of building defects occurring.

With traditional building, there was often a considerable safety margin inherent in the construction. With increased levels of insulation, this may be less so, and correct design and specification, as well as careful attention to good workmanship and supervision, may be necessary to ensure trouble free building. Also, in some situations, builders may prefer to select more robust forms of construction.

The scope and format of the guide

This guide explains the technical risks which may be associated with meeting the building regulation requirements for thermal insulation (conservation of fuel and power) for the major elements of the building:
☐ Roofs
☐ Walls
☐ Windows
☐ Floors

For Roofs and Floors, there are further sub-divisions within each element, often related to the insulation system or its position within the construction.

The report concentrates on loadbearing masonry, timber frame construction and, in some respects, profiled sheet cladding.

Within each subject area, explanations of the more important technical issues are highlighted and are followed by actions that could be taken to avoid the risk of failure.

Illustrations show construction principles and selected examples of good practice detailing. These examples are not exhaustive and designers and builders may have well established details using other materials that are equally suitable.

Throughout the guide, illustrations are numbered 1 to 94 and recommended actions, 101 to 483.

The information in the guide represents the recommendations of BRE on good construction practice associated with meeting the required thermal standards. It does not give guidance on which constructions meet particular U values.

The guide has been prepared with specific reference to Part L of the Building Regulations for England and Wales, but the potential technical risks and recommendations for avoiding action apply in principle throughout the United Kingdom.

This document is not an Approved Document under the Building Act 1984.

Technical risks related to heating

The provision of *heating* is not controlled by building regulations. However, it must be considered *in conjunction* with *thermal insulation* and *ventilation* in order to *avoid* the risk of *condensation.*

Ventilation and thermal insulation are covered by building regulations. This report also deals with cold bridging.

Condensation in unheated bedrooms

In two storey houses, insulation alone leads to increases in bedroom temperatures and may reduce the risk of condensation, because of the heat input from other parts of the dwelling.

In flats and bungalows, insulation has little effect on the conditions in unheated bedrooms, and **additonal heat will be required** in these rooms to avoid high relative humidities.

Condensation on internal surfaces

The thermal response of the roof, wall or floor is often affected by the position of the thermal insulation. High mass elements warm and cool slowly (slow response) and lightweight materials, rapidly (fast response). It is important to match the thermal response of the internal fabric with the type and pattern of heating to avoid the risk of surface condensation.

Where the thermal response is slow, constant low output heating systems are more appropriate; quick acting intermittently used heating systems are better suited to constructions with a fast thermal response.

The following potential technical risks are explained in the guide and recommended avoiding action given under each heading.

Roofs
PITCHED: TILE OR SLATE
- Condensation in the roof space
- Condensation in ventilation ducts within the roof space
- Condensation at cold bridges
- Fire and other hazards due to incorrect electrical installation
- Freezing of water in pipes and tanks
- Insulation becoming compressed where access is required

FLAT ROOFS
Cold deck
- Condensation within the roof space
- Condensation at cold bridges

Warm deck (sandwich)
- Condensation within the construction
- Fatigue of weatherproof membrane
- Insulant damaged by heat during construction
- Condensation at cold bridges
- Fire spread from melting or burning weatherproofing and combustible insulation

Warm deck (inverted)
- Degradation of the insulant
- Loss of insulation value due to rain cooling
- Condensation through chilling of the deck
- Condensation at cold bridges
- Abrasion of weatherproof membrane by grit

PITCHED: PROFILED SHEET
- Condensation within the construction
- Delamination between the roof sheet and the insulation
- Condensation at cold bridges
- Condensation on internal rainwater downpipes

Walls
- Rain penetration
- Frost attack on the outer leaf of a cavity wall
- Condensation at cold bridges
- Condensation within the construction
- Summer condensation with internal insulation
- Spread of fire gases in the wall cavity
- Fire due to combustible insulation
- Overheating of electrical cables
- Cracking of plaster due to shrinkage of blockwork
- Delamination of composite sheet cladding panels

Windows
- Deterioration of the edge seal in double glazed units
- Deformation of an undersized window frame
- Condensation on the external pane of double windows
- Increased condensation on single glazing when double glazing is used elsewhere
- Cold bridging of metal frames

Floors
CONCRETE GROUND FLOORS
Insulation below a screed
- Failure under load
- Damage in construction
- Damage from construction moisture
- Cold bridges at junctions
- Problems associated with services

Insulation below a board
- Uneven floor surface
- Damage from construction moisture
- Condensation within the construction
- Cold bridges at junctions
- Long term damage from water spillage

Insulation below a slab
- Failure due to floor loading
- Damage during construction
- Cold bridges at junctions
- Damage from construction moisture and rising damp

TIMBER SUSPENDED FLOORS
Insulation between the joists
- Uneven floor surface
- Cold bridges through the floor and at junctions
- Condensation within the construction
- Long term damage from water spillage
- Problems associated with services

UPPER FLOORS
Intermediate floors
- Cold bridges at junctions

Exposed soffit floors
- Cold bridges at junctions
- Condensation within the construction
- Long term damage from water spillage

1 ROOFS

The advice on avoiding risks when adding insulation to a roof has been well established for many years. However, the types of risk encountered depend largely on the roof form and type (ie pitched roof with tiled or profiled sheet finish, or flat roof). The three main roof types are discussed separately as follows:

□ **Pitched: tile or slate**
□ **Flat roofs**
□ **Pitched: profiled sheet**

PITCHED: TILE OR SLATE

Whether the insulation is placed at ceiling level, rafter level or, as with room in the roof designs, a combination of the two, the technical risks are essentially the same. The main risks are condensation in the roof space, cold bridging at the roof perimeter, fire hazards and freezing pipes and tanks.

Condensation in the roof space

Insulating rooms below or within the roof reduces the winter temperature in the roofspaces behind the insulation. Where water vapour from the dwelling reaches the cold roof areas, condensation will occur.

101 Ventilate the roof space to the outside air. Ventilation should be provided in accordance with BS 5250. Ensure the ventilation is not blocked by insulation at the eaves or sagging sarking felt. Do not locate flue outlets immediately below perimeter vents, or plastics gutters. Place a 3 to 4mm mesh across ventilation apertures to prevent the entry of insects. [1]

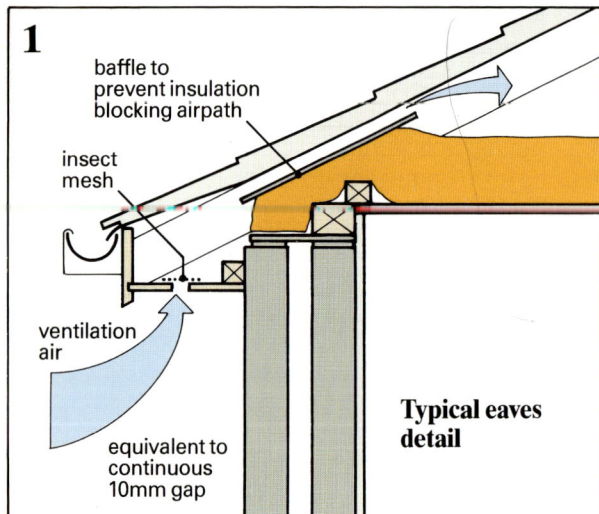

1

baffle to prevent insulation blocking airpath

insect mesh

ventilation air

equivalent to continuous 10mm gap

Typical eaves detail

102 Provide a vapour check (eg 500 gauge polythene) on the warm side of permeable insulation for rooms in the roof when insulation is placed at rafter level. [2]

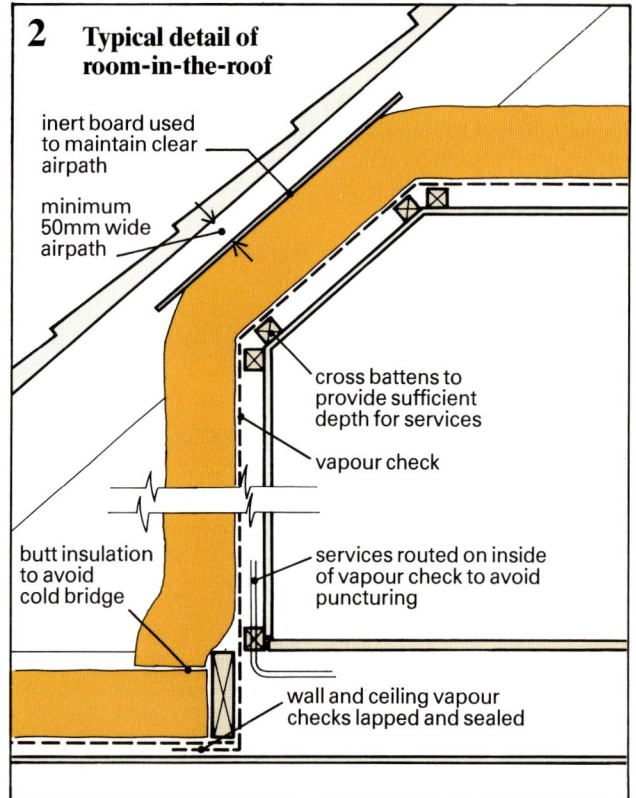

2 **Typical detail of room-in-the-roof**

inert board used to maintain clear airpath

minimum 50mm wide airpath

cross battens to provide sufficient depth for services

vapour check

butt insulation to avoid cold bridge

services routed on inside of vapour check to avoid puncturing

wall and ceiling vapour checks lapped and sealed

103 Fill all holes at ceiling level to block air paths. This restricts the amount of water vapour that enters the roof space from the habitable areas.

Unfilled holes in the ceiling allow large volumes of air, carrying water vapour, to enter the roof space.

The most important holes are around the roof hatch and pipes rising from the bathroom and linen cupboard. [3]

104 Provide a draughtseal at the loft hatch and bolts or catches to ensure it is compressed.

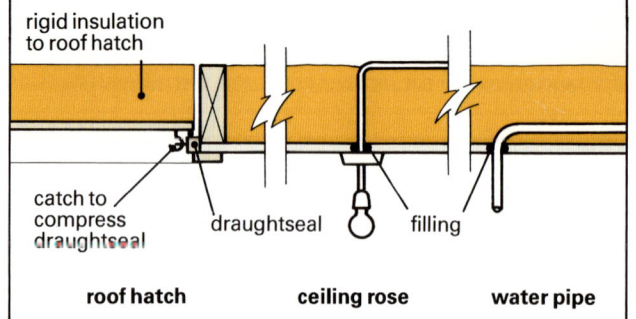

3 **Ceiling penetrations**

rigid insulation to roof hatch

catch to compress draughtseal

draughtseal

filling

roof hatch   **ceiling rose**   **water pipe**

Condensation in ventilation ducts within the roof space

The warm moist air extracted from kitchens and bathrooms cools when it passes through unheated roof spaces. If the air is cooled below its dew point, it will condense on the duct wall and drip back into the room.

105 Insulate ventilation ducts that pass through unheated spaces.

106 Avoid a cold bridge by adopting the following strategies:

- Carry the loft insulation over the wall plate and butt against the wall insulation. [4,5]
- Use only low density blocks where blockwork closes the cavity. Do not use bricks. [4]
- Cover the gap between ceiling joist and gable wall with insulation. [7]
- Extend the cold bridge path at the gable by "overlapping" the roof and wall insulation and using a low density block for the inner leaf. [7]

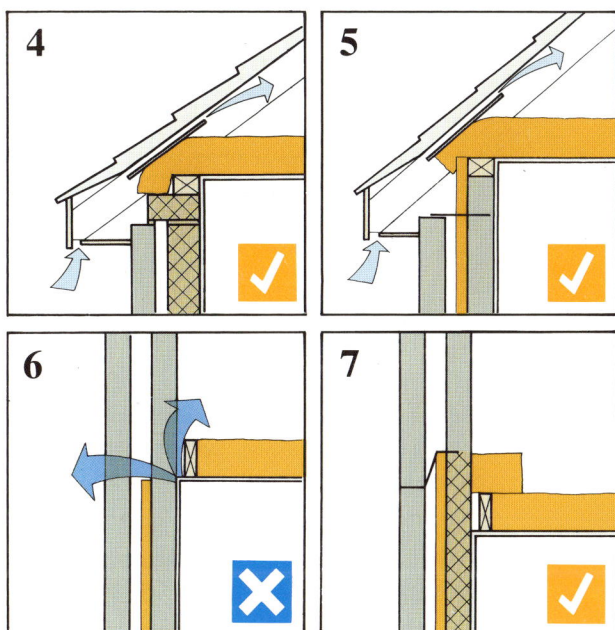

107 Route cables where they can dissipate heat (ie above the insulation) or use larger capacity cables (to allow for the effects of being covered with insulation). This is particularly important for cables serving cooker points and electric shower units (see Appendix).

108 Place PVC insulated cables in conduit or away from direct contact with expanded polystyrene insulants. This is to prevent the cable insulation becoming brittle as a result of migration of the plasticiser.

109 Avoid the use of recessed light fittings — they need to be cooled by a through airflow and this allows warm air from the house into the loft, with the risk of condensation. If used, make certain that no combustible insulation is placed above the fitting.

110 Locate pipes in heated spaces whenever possible, eg below loft insulation or below the ceiling.

111 Specify pipe insulation for all pipes, including overflows in unheated roof spaces (see Appendix). [8]

112 Insulate the top and sides of cold water cisterns in the roof space. Omit insulation from directly under the cistern, to allow warmth from below to reach the cistern base, but insulate the gap below the cistern base by turning up the loft insulation against the tank insulation. Try to include the rising main within the insulated enclosure for the tank. [8]

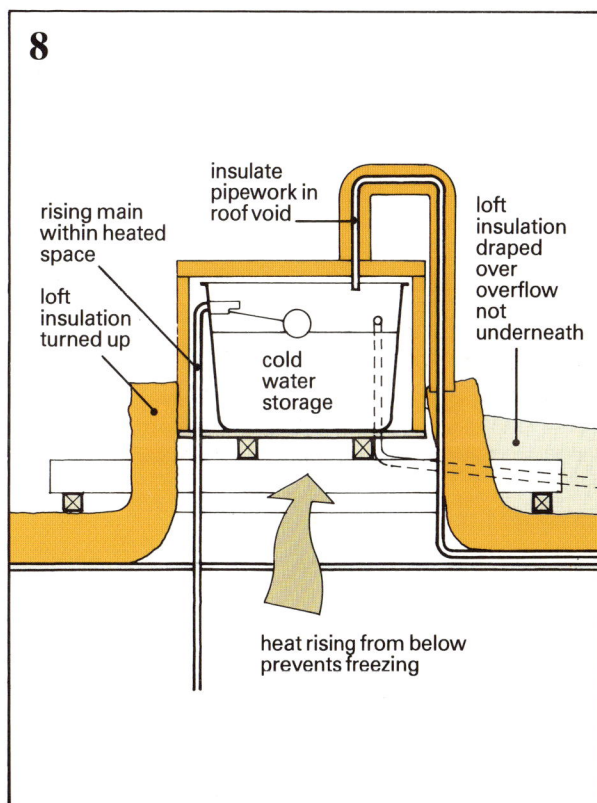

8

insulate pipework in roof void

rising main within heated space

loft insulation turned up

loft insulation draped over overflow not underneath

cold water storage

heat rising from below prevents freezing

113 Add battens to bring support for boarding, level with the top of the insulation (if the ceiling joists are not already of sufficient depth).

FLAT ROOFS

There are three alternative types of flat roof:

☐ **Cold deck**
☐ **Warm deck (sandwich)**
☐ **Warm deck (inverted)**

Each type has different technical risks associated with it. However, all roofs with internal rainwater downpipes can suffer from condensation on the downpipe (see 143). Uninsulated outlet boxes let into flat roofs are also at risk.

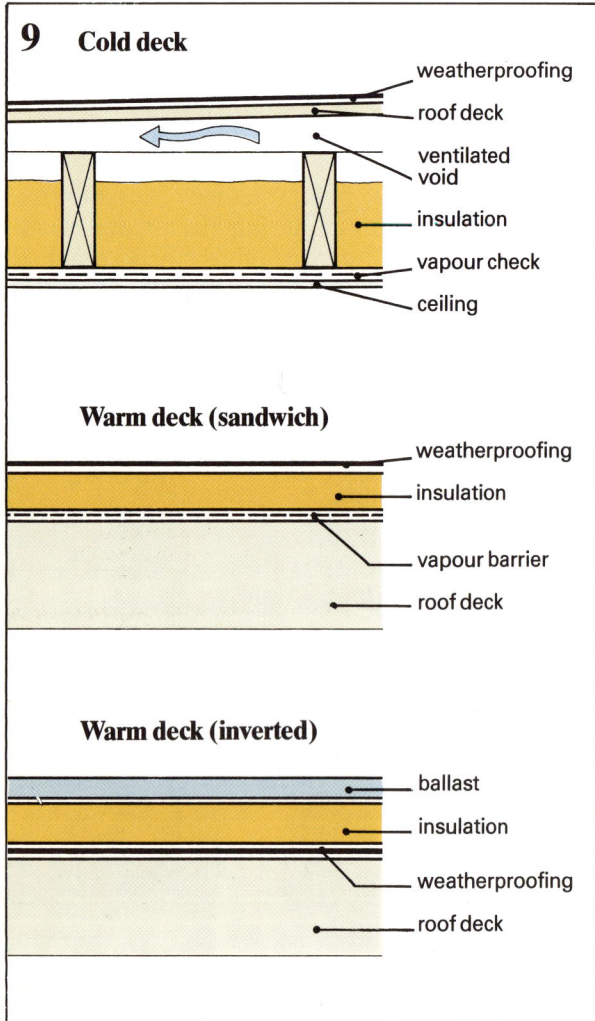

9 Cold deck

weatherproofing
roof deck
ventilated void
insulation
vapour check
ceiling

Warm deck (sandwich)

weatherproofing
insulation
vapour barrier
roof deck

Warm deck (inverted)

ballast
insulation
weatherproofing
roof deck

Cold deck

The insulation is placed at ceiling level with a void ventilated to the outside between the insulation and the deck.

Condensation within the roof space
The cold deck roof is regarded as a poor option in our temperate, humid climate. The risk of condensation can be high and is unpredicatable. Even when the roof is correctly designed, condensation may still occur due to lack of cross ventilation in windless conditions.

114 Provide an edge-sealed vapour check immediately below the insulation. Seal all holes where services pass through, but preferably avoid service penetrations (eg, batten out below the vapour check to accommodate services). [11]

115 In principle, insulation on both sides of a vapour barrier is undesirable. Where unavoidable, the greater thickness of insulation should be on the cold side.

116 Cross ventilate each and every void to the outside air. A minimum 50mm airspace above the insulation is required. [10] It is important to avoid solid strutting and to ventilate each discrete cavity. If cavity barriers or other obstructions block cross ventilation of any void, then a cold deck solution should not be used.

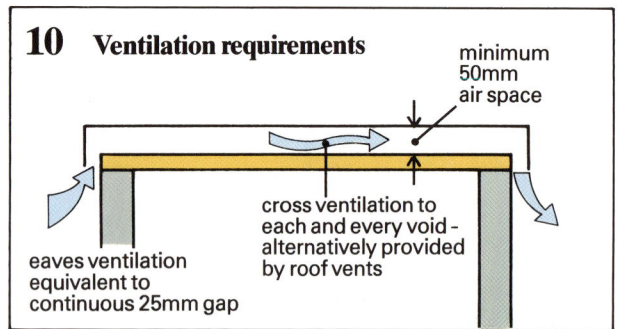

10 Ventilation requirements

minimum 50mm air space
cross ventilation to each and every void – alternatively provided by roof vents
eaves ventilation equivalent to continuous 25mm gap

117 Provide eaves ventilation on opposite sides of the roof, equivalent to a continuous 25mm gap. [10] For complex roof forms or low buildings in sheltered locations, the total free area of perimeter vents should be increased to 0.6% of the roof plan area. Do not locate flue outlets immediately below perimeter vents, or plastics gutters.

118 Place a 3 to 4mm mesh across ventilation apertures to prevent the entry of insects. [11]

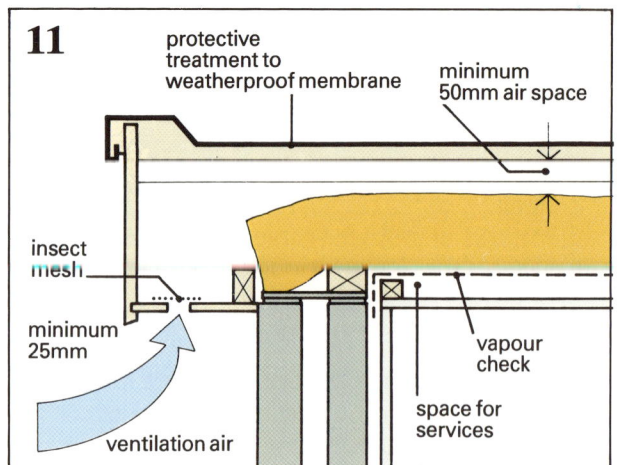

11

protective treatment to weatherproof membrane
minimum 50mm air space
insect mesh
minimum 25mm
vapour check
space for services
ventilation air

Condensation at cold bridges

119 "Overlap" roof and wall insulation. Ensure that paths of greatest heat loss provide a U value not greater than $1.2W/m^2K$ (see Appendix for method of calculation).

Warm deck (sandwich)

The insulation is placed above the roof deck, but below the weatherproof membrane. There should be no insulation below the deck. Ventilation is not required.

Condensation within the construction

120 Place a vapour barrier immediately below the insulation. The barrier should be fully supported with all joints bonded. When a 2 layer felt vapour barrier is used on timber boarded decks, the first layer should be nailed in place and the second fully bedded in hot bitumen. The vapour barrier should be turned up at the insulation perimeter and bonded to the weatherproof membrane. [12, 13] Where insulation is compressible and its thickness exceeds 25mm, separate supports should be provided to the weatherproof membrane.

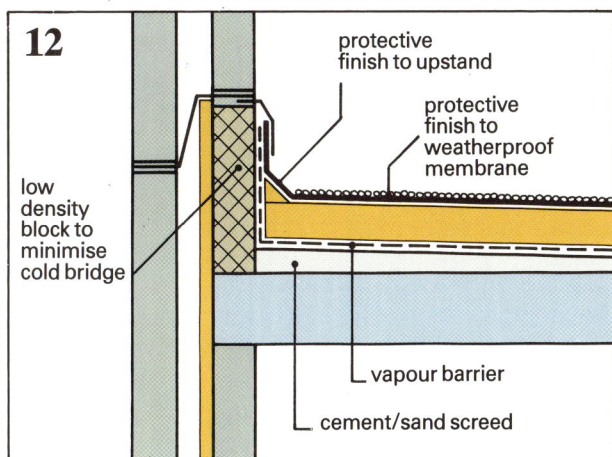

12

protective finish to upstand

protective finish to weatherproof membrane

low density block to minimise cold bridge

vapour barrier

cement/sand screed

Fatigue of weatherproof membrane

Placing insulation directly below the weatherproof membrane will increase the membrane's surface temperature fluctuations. On sunny days the insulation slows the heat flow to the deck causing a build up in the membrane's surface temperature. At night, in contrast, the lower rate of heat transfer from the building results in lower surface temperatures at the membrane as it loses heat by radiation to the night sky. The thermal stresses are increased with higher levels of insulation.

121 For built-up felt roofing, use a high tensile membrane to BS 747, Type 5, that is good at accommodating stresses and remains flexible over a wide temperature range.

122 Protect weatherproof membranes of bituminous felt with a solar reflective finish to reduce thermal stress. [12]

123 Select an insulant that minimises stress at board joins due to thermal movement.

124 For built-up felt roofing, use a partially bonded first layer. This spreads any stresses generated below the membrane over a larger membrane area. Use a sheathing felt below asphalt.

125 Provide sufficient falls for membranes of all kinds to ensure drainage and avoid ponding.

Insulant damaged by heat during construction

126 Protect expanded polystyrene with a layer of bitumen impregnated fibreboard, corkboard or vermiculite board, from the heat generated when laying asphalt or using hot bitumen. Consult the insulation manufacturer for the requirements for individual products.

Condensation at cold bridges

127 Maintain continuity of insulation at roof/wall junctions and at changes in level. [12, 13]

128 Check by calculation that no cold bridge path has a U value higher than $1.2W/m^2K$.

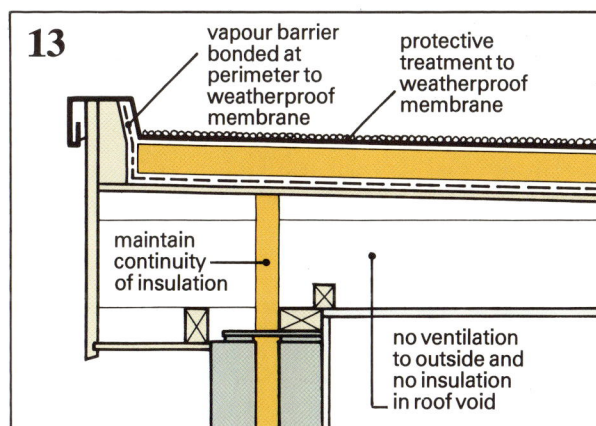

13

vapour barrier bonded at perimeter to weatherproof membrane

protective treatment to weatherproof membrane

maintain continuity of insulation

no ventilation to outside and no insulation in roof void

Fire spread from melting or burning weatherproofing and combustible insulation

A fire source inside the building may cause cellular plastics insulants and weatherproofing products to melt and/or decompose and generate flammable gases when they are laid directly onto unprotected metal decks. These and any molten materials, eg bitumen or polystyrene may penetrate joints in the roof deck and help spread the fire below.

129 Place a non-combustible layer (eg vermiculite or gypsum board) between the metal deck and expanded polystyrene, weatherproof membrane etc. Alternative methods of improved fire protection for insulated roof decks are available and could be usefully discussed with a fire expert.

Warm deck (inverted)

The insulation is placed above the weatherproof membrane. There should be no thermal insulation below the deck. [14, 15]

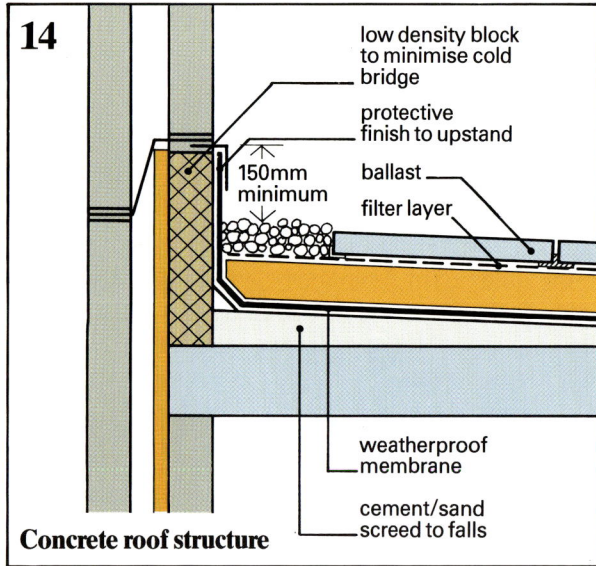

Concrete roof structure

Labels: low density block to minimise cold bridge; protective finish to upstand; 150mm minimum; ballast; filter layer; weatherproof membrane; cement/sand screed to falls

---

Degradation of the insulant
Being above the weatherproof membrane, the insulant is subject to freeze/thaw cycles, wetting and UV light.

130 Use an insulant with low water absorption which is frost resistant.

131 Protect plastics foam insulants from UV degradation. The ballast needed to prevent wind uplift provides UV protection.

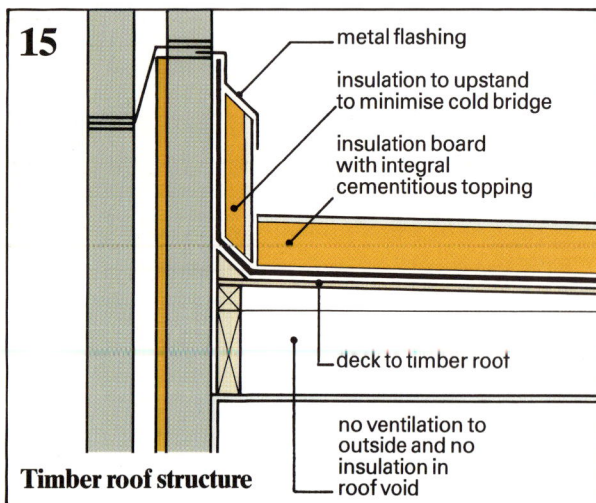

Timber roof structure

Labels: metal flashing; insulation to upstand to minimise cold bridge; insulation board with integral cementitious topping; deck to timber root; no ventilation to outside and no insulation in roof void

---

Loss of insulation value due to rain cooling
In the inverted roof, the weatherproof membrane remains close to room temperature at all times of the year. In winter, when rainwater flows over this relatively warm surface, there is an intermittent heat loss.

132 Use section A3 of the CIBSE Guide to calculate thermal insulation thickness, then increase insulation thickness by 20% to offset the intermittent cooling effect of rain.

Condensation through chilling of the deck
There is a risk of localised condensation on the underside of lightweight decks if melting snow or rainwater close to freezing percolates through the insulation layer and chills the deck. The risk is greatest where the internal temperature and the relative humidity are high. Concrete roof decks, because of their high thermal mass, are affected much less by chilling and do not normally suffer from surface condensation.

133 Ensure that the thermal resistance of the construction beneath the weatherproofing is at least $0.15 m^2 K/W$. Tightly butt joint insulation boards, and trim tightly around projections and at upstands.

Condensation at cold bridges

134 "Overlap" wall and roof insulation. [17, 18, 19] Ensure that paths of greatest heat loss provide a U value not greater than $1.2 W/m^2 K$.

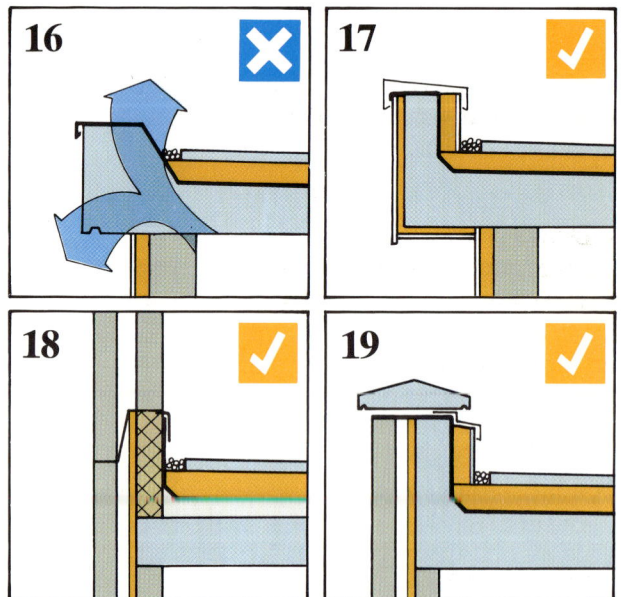

Abrasion of weatherproof membrane by grit
Grit washed down between the insulation boards can cause abrasion and eventual puncture of single layer membranes.

135 Place a suitable geotextile membrane above the insulation, but below the ballast; turn the filter membrane up at upstands. [14]

PITCHED: PROFILED SHEET

There are two alternative positions for the insulation in profiled sheet roofs:

☐ On the inner face, with a ventilated cavity above (**Type A**), [20, 21], or

☐ In contact with the profiled sheet (**Type B**).

Panels with the insulation in contact with the sheet can be formed by foaming (composite panels) or using specially shaped insulants to match the sheet profile. [22]

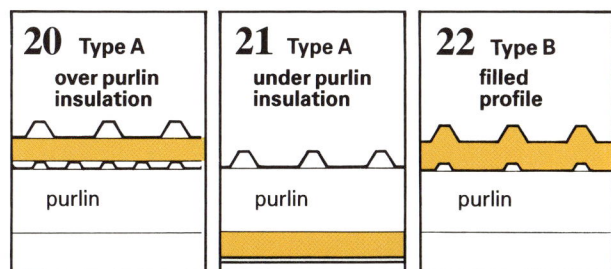

20 Type A
over purlin
insulation

purlin

21 Type A
under purlin
insulation

purlin

22 Type B
filled
profile

purlin

Condensation within the construction

This is a substantial risk with Type A roofs. Condensate invariably forms on the inner face of the outer sheet due to night sky radiation and sometimes freezes there. Condensate can saturate the insulation and corrode fixings and the edges of metal sheet. Condensate will eventually drip onto ceilings and into the building.

136 Use a Type B roof, ie avoid an airspace directly below the outer sheet by filling all voids with impervious insulation.

137 Use Type A roofs only where it is possible to:

● Detail the roof so that condensate drains to the eaves gutter, ie by means of a breather membrane. The natural drainage paths should not be blocked by purlins, roof lights etc.

● Extract at source any moist air produced inside the building.

138 Ensure that fixings at laps are made as high as possible in the lower sheet and the seal is placed immediately below the fixings. This minimizes the amount of condensate that can collect between the sheets. [23, 24]

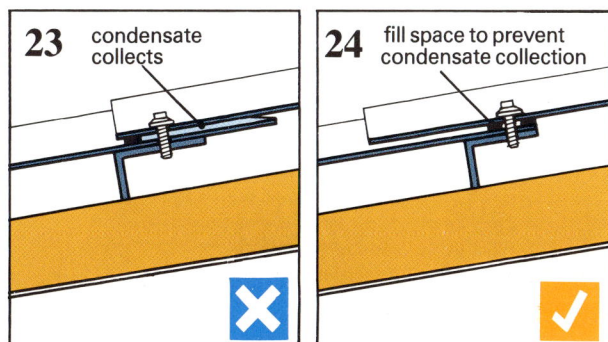

23 condensate collects

24 fill space to prevent condensate collection

Delamination between the roof sheet and the insulation

With composite panels of Type B construction, an inadequate bond during manufacture between insulation and the outer sheet may be broken due to the extreme thermal movements in the outer sheet. This results in bowing and possibly condensation in the newly formed voids.

139 Seek assurance from the manufacturer that there is an adequate bond between the upper sheet and the insulation. Dark colours should not be used.

Condensation at cold bridges

Purlins and fixings commonly link inner and outer metal components and these can rust. Internal gutters are often uninsulated. Condensation can also occur at panel joints between insulation in Type B roofs.

140 Limit relative humidity by extracting moisture at source.

141 Specify insulated gutters, or design the roof to fall to external eaves gutters. Insulation should be in contact with the gutter and be of closed cell construction.

142 Specify Type B roofs that have either:

☐ An overlap at the joints between insulation boards [26], or

☐ A continuous vapour seal in the joint to drain condensate into a gutter. [27]

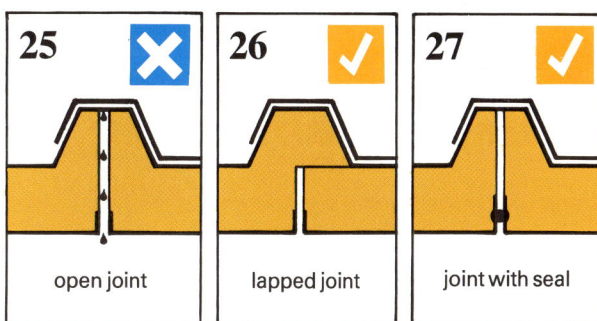

25 open joint

26 lapped joint

27 joint with seal

Condensation on internal rainwater downpipes

The walls of rainwater downpipes and other pipes that penetrate the roof (ie soil and vent pipes) present a cold surface on which moisture from the room air can condense.

143 See that all internal downpipes and pipes that penetrate the roof are insulated. Pipes over 50mm diameter should have insulation at least 16mm thick. Use an insulant that will not absorb any condensate that forms on the pipe. BS 6700 recommends a vapour barrier around the insulation.

2 WALLS

There is a wide range of constructions that can meet U values below 0.6 W/m²K. The main risks are rain penetration, durability, condensation at cold bridges and within the construction and spread of fire gases in cavities.

The technical risks outlined in Table 1 need to be considered whatever level of insulation is adopted.

Rain penetration

Rainwater will penetrate the outer leaves of masonry walls under certain conditions of driving rain.

Total resistance to rain penetration can only be achieved by cladding the wall (eg with tile hanging, timber boarding, uPVC siding or an impervious cladding).

Clear cavities, if properly constructed, can prevent rainwater passing from outer to inner leaves. Filled cavities provide adequate resistance to rain penetration, provided the walls are built and the insulation installed as indicated in the following pages.

Wall construction	Insulation position	Type of insulation or wall finish	Summary of main risks
SOLID MASONRY cladding or render	external	Combustible cladding or insulation	• Spread of fire over cladding • Spread of fire gases where cavities exist, abutting insulation
		Render	• Rain penetration through shrinkage cracks
	insulating masonry	Render on combustible insulation	• Integrity of render in case of fire • Integrity of plastics fixings
		Fairfaced masonry	• Rain penetration
optional cladding or render	internal / vapour check	Internal insulation	• Interstitial condensation if vapour check is missing • Spread of fire gases where cavities exist, abutting insulation • Contribution to fire from burning insulation • Risk of summer condensation on back of vapour check • Overheating of electrical cables in insulation
UNFILLED CAVITY	internal	Fairfaced masonry	• Rain penetration if wall not properly constructed
		Internal insulation	• Spread of fire gases where cavities exist, abutting insulation • Contribution to fire from burning insulation • Cold bridging at openings and junctions with internal walls and floors • Overheating of electrical cables in insulation
	insulating masonry	Insulating masonry	• Cracking of plaster due to blockwork shrinkage • Cold bridging at openings
CAVITY INSULATION	partial cavity fill	Fairfaced masonry	• Rain penetration if wall not properly constructed or cavity insulation not correctly installed • Cold bridging at openings
	full cavity fill	Partial cavity fill	• Spread of fire gases in cavity, eg from combustible insulation
		Full cavity fill	• Increased vulnerability to frost and/or sulphate attack if outer leaf painted
TIMBER FRAME option of brickwork or cladding	between studs / vapour check	Insulation between studs	• Rain penetration if wall not properly constructed • Interstitial condensation if vapour check is missing • Fire spread if cavity between timber frame and outer cladding or brick skin is penetrated • Overheating of electrical cables in insulation
	as sheathing to timber frame	Sheathing insulation	• Rain penetration if wall not properly constructed • Fire spread in cavity between insulation and cladding or brick skin • Condensation risk from impermeable cladding applied direct to the outer face
SHEET CLADDING	in the cavity	Combustible insulation adjacent to cavity	• Spread of fire gases in cavity • Condensation in cavity • Cold bridging at metal to metal contacts
	composite construction	Composite construction	• Delamination between insulation and outer sheets • Cold bridging at metal to metal contacts • Contribution to fire from burning insulation

Table 1 Summary of risk for a range of common constructions

201 To minimise the risk, follow the procedure below to determine the local exposure to wind driven rain, and select a suitable wall construction, carefully considering the design, detailing, workmanship and materials to be used.

Determine the degree of exposure

202 The map shows the variation in exposure across the country, based on data in BSI Draft for Development DD93 and related to the exposure categories defined in BS 5628:Part 3.

The contour lines dividing categories have been determined from an analysis of the worst likely spell of wind driven rain, occurring on average every 3 years, plotted on a 10km grid. The analysis is based on the "worst case" for each geographical area, ie the wall has a clear line of sight to open country and is facing the prevailing wind. Examples are a gable wall on the edge of a suburban site facing the prevailing wind and with a clear view of open countryside, one which is set back from the edge but also has a clear view of open country between other houses, or walls of a tall building projecting above other buildings within an urban area.

203 Buildings that have no clear line of sight of open country (ie they are sheltered by surrounding buildings and trees) can be considered to be located in an exposure category ranging from one lower in nominally *Sheltered* parts of the country to two lower in *Very severe* zones.

204 Because the exposure categories overlap in BS 5628:Part 3, the contour lines represent only an approximate division between zones. However, the map does provide a simple starting point for selecting a suitable form of construction. **[28]** For a more detailed analysis using larger scale maps, refer to DD93.

28   **Map showing categories of exposure to wind driven rain**

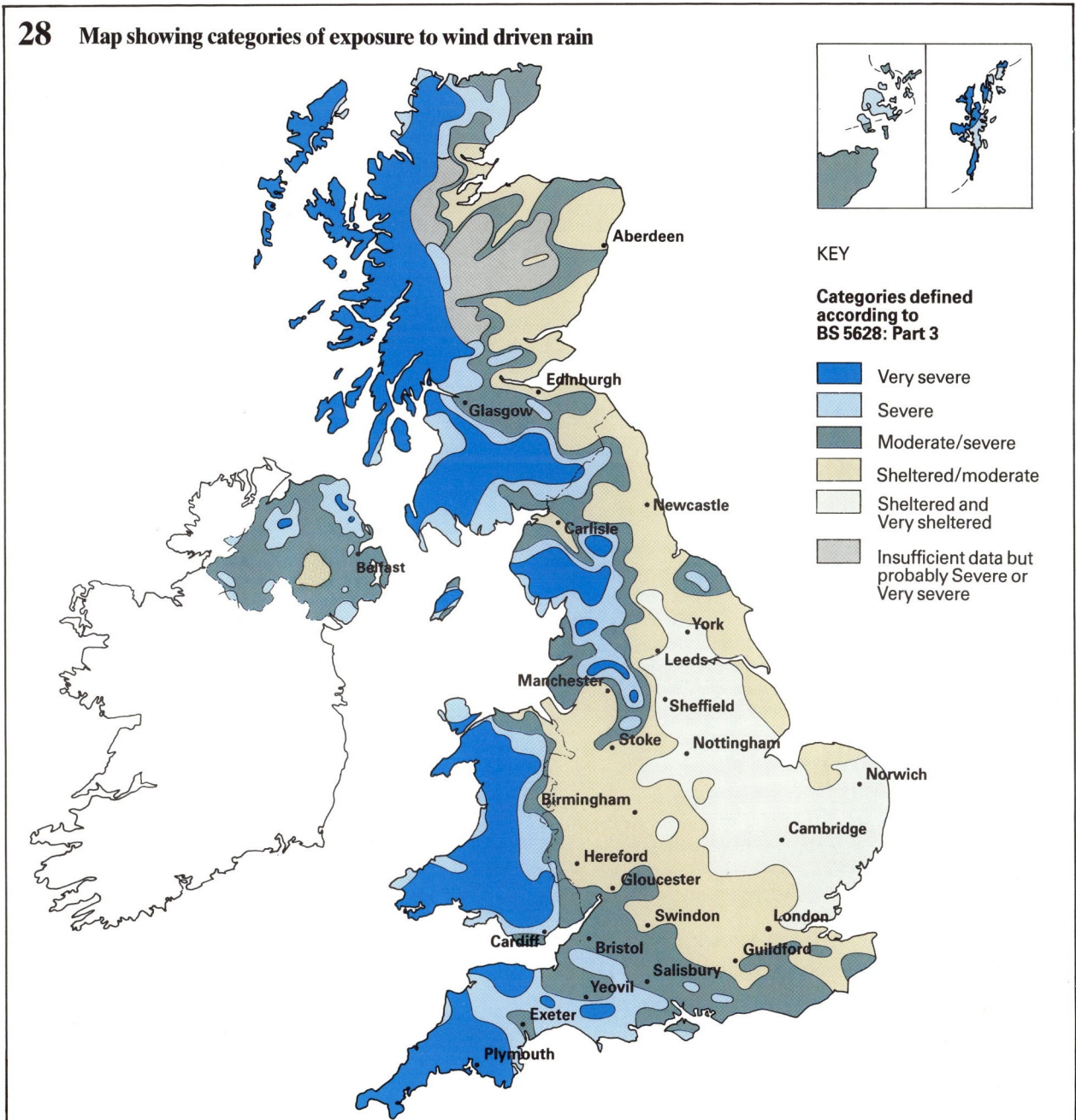

KEY

Categories defined according to BS 5628: Part 3

- Very severe
- Severe
- Moderate/severe
- Sheltered/moderate
- Sheltered and Very sheltered
- Insufficient data but probably Severe or Very severe

Select a suitable form of construction

205 A range of common wall constructions and the highest exposure category for which they are suitable is given in Table 2. To be suitable for the exposure levels shown, the walls must comply with good practice recommendations given in British Standards and BBA Certificates. For masonry walls, the table assumes that walls comply with the items listed in Table 3.

206 If the designer departs from the detailing items listed in Table 3, or the standard of workmanship cannot be relied upon, the exposure rating of the wall should be downgraded. Table 4 provides some advice on the factors that affect the exposure rating — other factors are discussed below.

Other factors affecting the exposure rating

207 Rendering can enhance the rain resistance of a wall, but it is *essential* to ensure *correct specification* and *application* to an appropriate backing material to minimise cracking, which may otherwise reduce the effectiveness of render against rain penetration.

208 Render over external insulation when correctly applied can provide very high resistance to rain penetration. However, rendering on insulation is subject to greater fluctuations in temperature and impact damage than when applied directly to masonry. The following have been found to minimise cracking:

- Reinforcing the render with a mesh.
- Providing movement joints at maximum 6m intervals.
- Using a white or light coloured finish.
- Using a render either incorporating a polymer emulsion or with a flexible topcoat.

209 Protective design features can greatly reduce the amount of rainwater running down the outer face of the wall. Deep overhanging eaves and verges are features that reduce the amount of rain that falls on a wall and so help to keep it dry. Projecting sills and overhanging string courses throw water clear of the wall.

210 Absorbent masonry can limit the amount of rain that penetrates the wall by absorbing it. The periods of wind driven rain are usually short enough to prevent the outer leaf becoming completely saturated, and intervening dry periods allow moisture to evaporate. In contrast, low absorbency bricks with a smooth impervious finish can be more susceptible to rain penetration. During heavy rain, water runs down the surface and can rapidly penetrate the outer leaf through small cracks and unfilled perpends.

Maximum exposure category	Suitable wall constructions	Notes
Very severe	Any wall with cladding of metal, plastics, slate, tile hanging, timber boarding or similar	Assumes flashings are correctly detailed and insulation directly behind the cladding is faced with a breather membrane
	50mm clear cavity wall with a rendered finish, including timber frame	
Severe	Fairfaced cavity wall with an unfilled clear cavity at least 50mm wide	Applies to masonry or timber framed inner leaf. May also be used in certain *Very severe* locations as defined by map (see BS 5628)
	Fairfaced cavity masonry wall with partial fill and a residual clear cavity at least 50mm wide	With a 50mm residual clear cavity and correct installation, partial fill can be expected to perform as well as an unfilled cavity
	Fairfaced cavity masonry wall with full fill (except UF foam)	Check BBA certificate for any restriction to use. Minor imperfections in workmanship may assume greater significance than with a clear cavity and will reduce the exposure rating
Moderate/severe	Fairfaced cavity masonry wall with any cavity insulation	Assumes installation in accordance with relevant BS or BBA certificate
Sheltered	Unrendered solid masonry wall	Minimum 330mm thick With rendered solid walls, the resistance to driving rain depends on the type and thickness of masonry (see Table 11 in BS 5628: Part 3). Highest exposure category for rendered solid walls is *Severe*

Note: assumes all masonry walling complies with BS 5628: Part 3 and cavity insulation is installed in accordance with the relevant BBA Certificate, or BS 5618 for UF foam (see Table 3).

Table 2 Maximum exposure categories for locally exposed wall constructions (see 202)

Design requirements (BS 5628: Part 3)

- The following types of cavity should be at least 50mm wide:
  - an unfilled cavity
  - a residual clear cavity with partial fill
  - a structural cavity with full fill construction

  Wider cavities reduce the likelihood of rain penetration.
- Provide cavity trays and dpc s at all interruptions to the cavity so they direct to the outside any water that enters the cavity.
- Cavity trays should rise 150mm within the cavity, be self supporting or fully supported and have joints lapped and sealed.
- Provide cavity trays with stop ends.
- Provide weepholes at no more than 1m centres.
- Provide continuous cavity trays over short piers between closely spaced openings.
- For complicated openings, provide clear drawings and use of pre-formed profiles.
- Projections at sills, copings and below cladding to be at least 50mm and incorporate a throating.
- Mortar joints should be tooled, either bucket handle, or weathered.
- Use a mortar mix and strength compatible with the strength and type of masonry units.

Workmanship requirements (BS 5628: Part 3)

- Well fill all mortar joints, particularly perpends.
- Build the outer leaf ahead of the inner leaf (except for partial cavity fill fixed against the inner leaf).

- Strike off projecting mortar from the inside of the outer leaf.
- Keep the cavity free of mortar droppings and other debris.
- Position wall ties centrally in the cavity and slope them downwards towards the outer leaf.
- Project vertical dpc s 25mm beyond cavity closers at openings.

Additional points for built-in cavity insulation

- Closely butt boards and batts to avoid gaps at the joints.
- Remove mortar droppings from the exposed edges of the insulation.
- Take the insulation to the top of the wall, or protect with a cavity tray.
- Follow the installation procedure given in the BBA Certificate and the manufacturer's literature.
- For partial fill, use the special ties or clips recommended by the manufacturer.
- For full fill, build the cavity width within the specified tolerances — to avoid compression or sagging of the insulation.

Additional points for installers of cavity fill systems.

- The builder and installer should liaise on design, particularly in *Severe* and *Very severe* exposure categories.
- Check that the necessary design and constructional standards have been achieved particularly in respect of the information given in BS 8208: Part 1.
- Ensure the cavity is completely filled.

Table 3   Design and workmanship requirements

Possible changes to wall built to BS 5628: Part 3		Effect of changes on exposure rating of the wall
Add cladding to wall	↑	Can improve the exposure rating of the clad area to *Very severe*
Ground floor fairfaced walls with cladding added to upper floors	↑	Improves the exposure rating of the fairfaced wall by up to two categories
Increase clear cavity width, or width of full cavity fill from 50 to 100mm	↑	Increase of up to two categories in the exposure rating of the wall
Detailing and workmanship to BS 5628: Part 3	=	No change (see Table 3)
Installation of cavity insulation in accordance with BBA Certificate or British Standard	=	No change (see Table 3)
Workmanship less than BS 5628: Part 3, or installation not to BBA Certificate requirements	↓	Reduces exposure rating of the wall. More critical when insulation is placed in the cavity
Strong mortar for the wall generally, flush detailing at sills, parapets etc.	↓	These factors reduce the exposure rating of the wall
Recessed mortar joints	↓	Consider only in *Sheltered* or *Very sheltered* areas

Table 4   Factors that effect the exposure rating of the wall

Frost attack on the outer leaf of a cavity wall

The main factors affecting frost attack are the degree of exposure to wind driven rain combined with the frequency of sub-zero temperatures and the frost resistance of the masonry.

The changes in temperature and moisture content due to increased insulation are small and there is little evidence that insulated walls with a fairfaced outer leaf have a higher incidence of frost damage than uninsulated walls. However, walls with a painted finish or cracked rendering are more susceptible to frost attack.

211 For all walls, use masonry with sufficient frost resistance for the degree of exposure to wind driven rain and freezing temperatures. Clay bricks should be designated frost resistant (F in BS 3921:1985) for masonry where the combination of exposure and frost incidence are exceptionally severe. London Brick Company have defined such masonry as having a clear uninterrupted line of sight to long stretches of open country (ie no protection from trees, hedges or buildings) and the site is located over 90m above sea level and receives on average over 60 days of frost incidence and 1000mm of rainfall annually.

212 Defective render is susceptible to frost attack and full cavity fill can be expected to increase the rate of deterioration. When considering rendering onto clay bricks that have a soluble salt designation N (Normal as determined in BS 3921) in exposed situations, a sulphate resisting cement should be used in the base coat of the render (see BS 5628:Part 3:Table 13).

213 Avoid painted finishes on fairfaced masonry as this can impair the ability of the wall to dry out and the risk of frost damage is increased. The combination of a painted finish and full cavity fill can significantly increase the risk of frost damage.

Condensation at cold bridges

If a dense element bridges the insulation layer, or the insulation is interrupted, the indoor surface temperature may locally fall below dew point leading to condensation, staining and mould growth.

214 Maintain an adequate internal surface temperature by ensuring that no part of the external wall has a U value greater than $1.2W/m^2K$.

Window and door openings

215 Cold bridges can occur at window and door reveals and heads and at window sills. There are two alternative strategies for minimising the risks:
- Position the window frame within the depth of the opening so that the full width of wall insulation can be continued up to the frame, or
- Add sufficient insulation to decrease the U value to $1.2 W/m^2K$ (eg insulated cavity closer, insulated lining to soffit, or box lintel with insulation). [30]

Junctions with partitions and floors

216 It is only with internal insulation that cold bridging is likely to occur at these junctions. To avoid complicated detailing, it is advisable to use a block with a sufficiently low density that the wall construction achieves a U value of 1.2 or better where the insulated lining is omitted. Check that loadbearing capacity and sound insulation requirements are not impaired. [29]

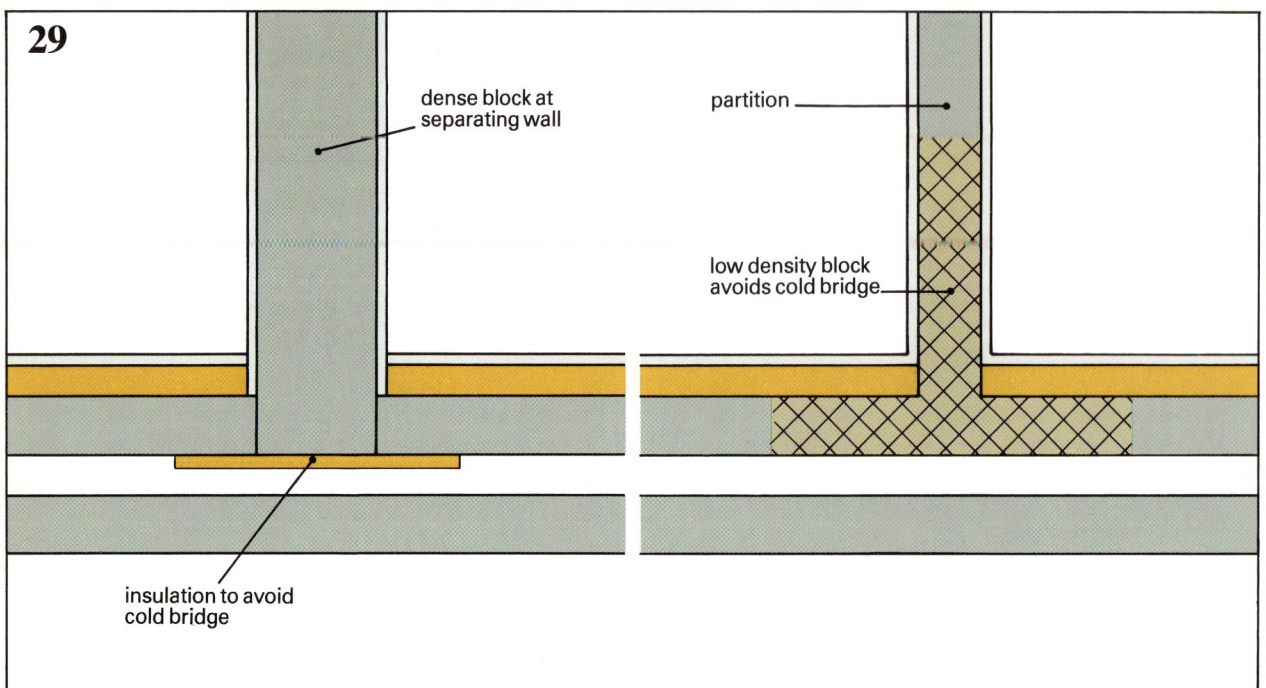

29

dense block at separating wall

partition

low density block avoids cold bridge

insulation to avoid cold bridge

30 Risk of cold bridge

lintel	jamb	sill

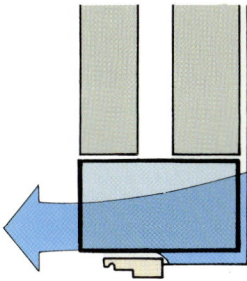 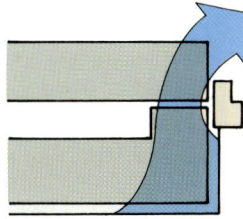 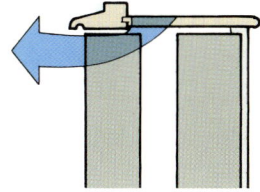

Avoiding action

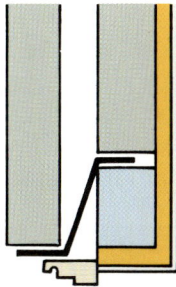 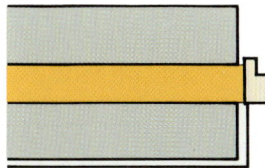 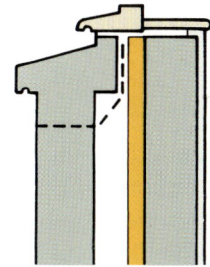

1 Continue internal insulation to the frame (applies also to external insulation)

 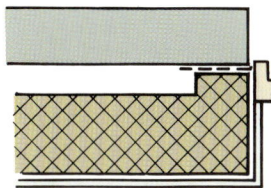 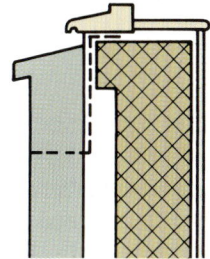

2 Overlap window frame and insulating blockwork

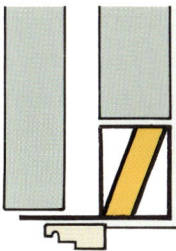 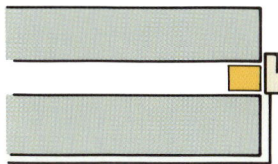 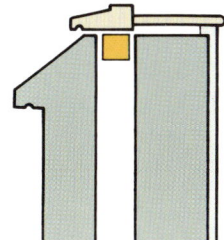

3 Use box lintel with insulation and use insulating cavity closers

 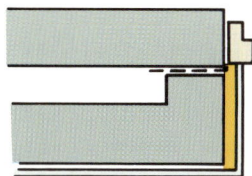 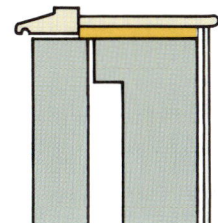

4 If frame placed forward, insulate soffit, reveal and under sill

Condensation within the construction*

Where insulation is located internally, moisture laden air may condense within the wall on the cold side of the insulation. In a masonry cavity wall with cavity or internal insulation, condensation usually occurs in the outer leaf. As this not likely to be a problem, a vapour check is not necessary.

217 Provide the means of removing water vapour at source, eg install extract fans or passive extract systems in kitchens and bathrooms.

218 Avoid the use of impermeable cladding on walls with a vapour check on the inside, unless there is a ventilated cavity.

219 If possible, introduce a cavity ventilated to the outside on the cold side of the insulation. This is especially important with impermeable cladding such as metal sheet.

220 Use a breather membrane to BS4016 behind tile hanging or similar cladding. Do not use polythene or building paper. Where a wall contains timber or other materials that are adversely affected by damp, and the thermal insulation is fitted between the studs, provide a vapour check on the warm side of the insulation. Timber and timber products outside the vapour check may need to be treated with preservative to bring them to the required level of durability.

221 Pay particular attention to maintaining the continuity of the vapour check at joints and junctions between elements and where services penetrate. Try to locate services so they do not penetrate the vapour check.

Summer condensation with internal insulation

In solid masonry walls with insulated linings orientated from ESE through South to WSW, solar driven vapour pressure can cause condensation on the back (ie the outside) of the vapour check.

222 Introduce a cavity ventilated to the outside, either:
- Between the masonry and insulation, or
- Within the wall (ie cavity wall construction).

Alternatively, clad the outside of the wall (ie tile hanging, timber boarding etc).

*BS 5250 can be used to assess the severity of condensation in constructions.

Spread of fire gases in the wall cavity

Smoke and fire gases can spread through hidden voids and cavities in the construction.

Cavity insulation

223 Where combustible insulation is placed in the cavity of a masonry wall, there is no significant deterioration in its fire resistance. Spread of fire can be prevented by placing cavity barriers at the head of walls and around openings.

Internal insulation

224 Seal the junctions of insulation/plasterboard laminates with floors, ceilings and adjoining walls using timber battens or continuous ribbons of plaster. This can also reduce air leakage and thus save energy.

External insulation and sheet cladding

225 Install cavity barriers at a minimum of 2 storey intervals where a cavity is formed by the overcladding of combustible external insulation, and provide cavity barriers around windows. [31]

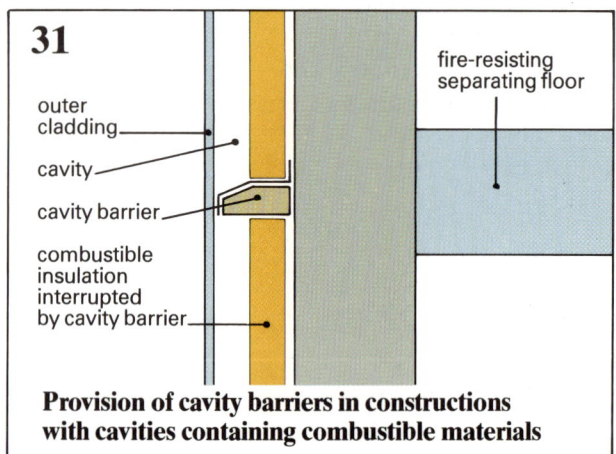

31

outer cladding

cavity

cavity barrier

combustible insulation interrupted by cavity barrier

fire-resisting separating floor

Provision of cavity barriers in constructions with cavities containing combustible materials

Timber framed construction

226 Install cavity barriers at junctions of separating walls and floors in order to maintain the full fire resistance of the divisions.

227 Install cavity barriers at the head of the cavity and around all openings.

Fire due to combustible insulation

Where combustible insulants are added to the face of a wall, they present a fire hazard and must be protected by materials that can restrict their contribution to a fire and satisfy the requirements for surface spread of flame.

Internal insulation

228 Protect combustible internal insulation with a facing material that can prevent involvement of the insulation for 15 minutes under the standard fire conditions of BS 476: Part 8 or 20 and meet the flame spread requirements for surfaces, as necessary (BS 476: Parts 6 and 7).

229 Protective material should be mechanically fixed through the insulation to prevent premature collapse (eg nine nails or screws per 2.4m x 1.2m board are recommended).

External insulation
230 Where combustible insulation boards are rendered:
- Select a render that can prevent active fire involvement of the insulant and which can, in combination with it, meet a Class O surface rating if required.
- A render, reinforced with metal mesh, should be mechanically fixed through the insulation, using some non-combustible fixings, to prevent premature collapse of the render.

Overheating of electrical cables
All electrical cables give off heat when in use. Where cables are covered by thermal insulation they may overheat, with risk of short circuit or fire.

Timber frame and internal insulation
231 Route cables where they will not be covered by insulation. If this is not possible, the cables should be suitably derated — this may involve using larger sized cables, especially where they serve cooker points and electric shower units (see Appendix). [32, 33]

232 Locate PVC insulated cables away from direct contact with expanded polystyrene insulation or in conduit where they pass through it.

---

32   **Internal insulation**

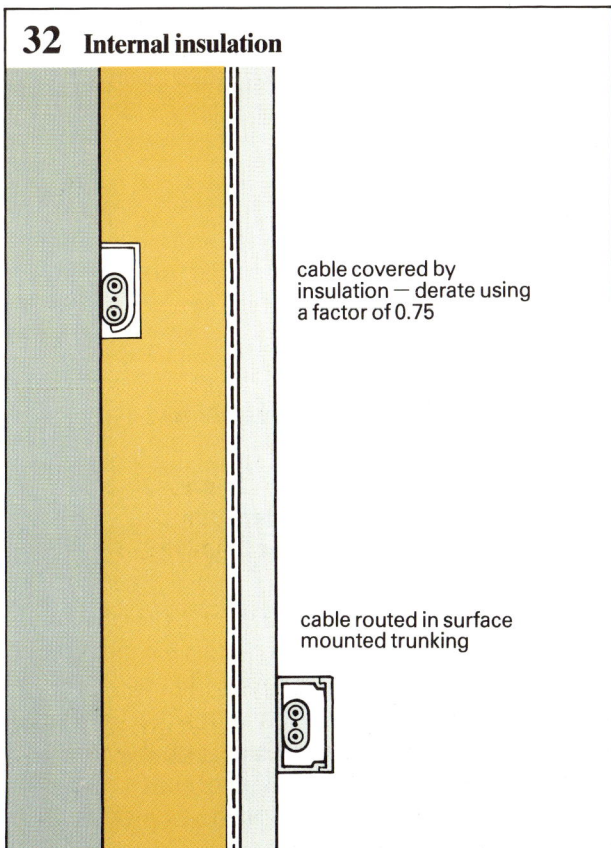

cable covered by insulation — derate using a factor of 0.75

cable routed in surface mounted trunking

---

33   **Timber frame construction**

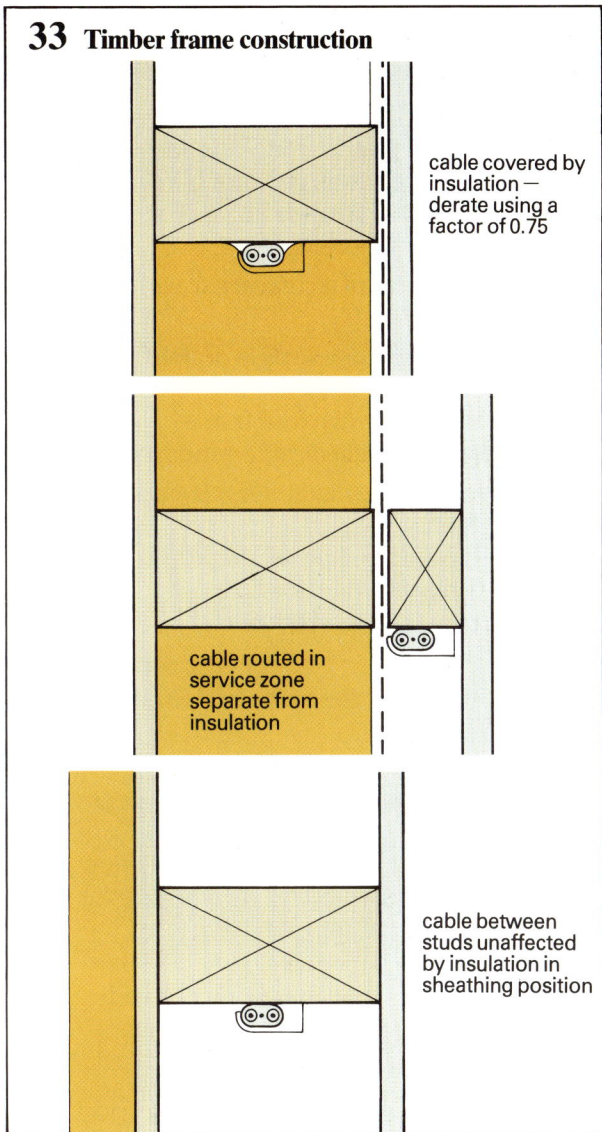

cable covered by insulation — derate using a factor of 0.75

cable routed in service zone separate from insulation

cable between studs unaffected by insulation in sheathing position

---

Cracking of plaster due to shrinkage of blockwork
Lightweight insulating concrete blocks have a relatively high rate of drying shrinkage. If the blocks are wet when a plaster finish is applied, the subsequent shrinkage of the blocks can cause the plaster to crack.

---

233 Keep blocks dry or use dry lining. This avoids possible difficulties with wet plaster finishes.

Delamination of composite sheet cladding panels
An inadequate bond between the insulation and the metal cladding during manufacture may be broken by the thermal movement of the outer sheet. This results in bowing and possibly condensation in the newly formed voids.

---

234 Seek assurance from the manufacturer that there is an adequate bond between the insulation and the outer sheet of the cladding panel.

3 WINDOWS

Proposed revisions to building regulations include new provisions for simple trade-offs between areas of double glazing and wall and roof U values. This makes it likely that double glazing will be installed more widely in new dwellings.

The three main areas of technical risk with double glazing are:

☐ **Deterioration of edge seals** in double glazed units
☐ **Deformation of undersized frames**
☐ **Condensation within double windows**.

Two problems may be made worse by increased use of double glazing:

☐ **Increased condensation on single glazing** when double glazing is used elsewhere
☐ **Cold bridging of metal frames**.

Deterioration of the edge seal in double glazed units

The main risk is from prolonged wetting of the edge seal when water is trapped behind the glazing bead. Most edge seals will also deteriorate if exposed to sunlight, and there may be compatibility problems between the edge seal and the glazing materials used.

301 Use a glazing method that either provides adequate drainage and ventilation, or has a solid bedding using a water vapour permeable sealant. Avoid methods that rely on perfect workmanship or frequent maintenance to prevent premature failure of the edge seal. *Glazing techniques for insulating glass units* by the GGF gives more detailed advice on preferred glazing methods.

302 Use rebates that are at least 15mm deep to ensure full coverage of the edge seal. [34,35]

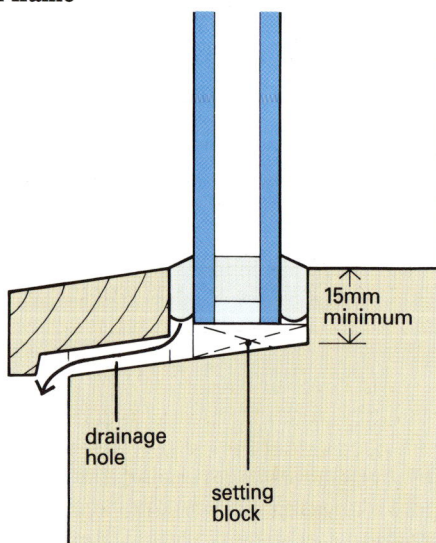

34 Drained and ventilated glazing method — timber frame

15mm minimum

drainage hole

setting block

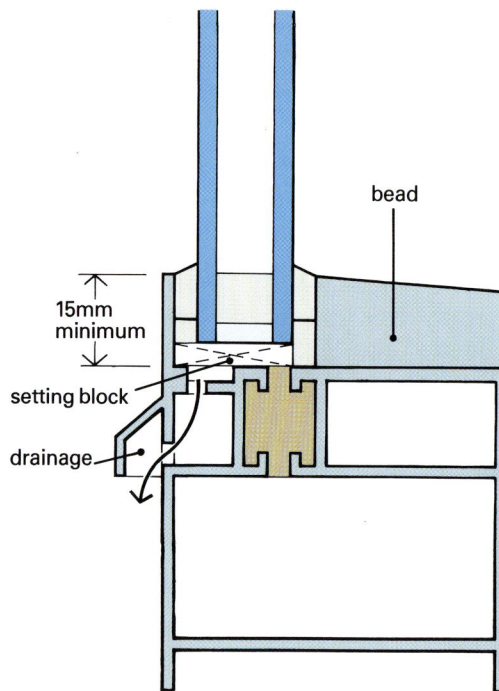

35 Drained and ventilated glazing method — uPVC or metal frame with internal bead

bead

15mm minimum

setting block

drainage

303 Use sealed units to BS 5713 and Kitemarked. Check with the manufacturer of the sealed units that the edge seal is compatible with the proposed glazing materials.

Deformation of an undersized window frame

Some lightweight window frames designed for single glazing are not robust enought for the extra weight of double glazed units. Frames may deflect repeatedly under wind gusting and may cause glazing units to crack or seals to be broken.

304 Use windows designed to accommodate multi-glazed units. Do not exceed manufacturers' recommended limits on sash weights and dimensions.

Condensation on the external pane of double windows

This can be slow to clear and results in unacceptable fogging and eventual deterioration of lower frame members.

305 Draughtstrip the inner window to provide an impervious airtight seal. This restricts the movement of moist internal air into the cavity. Do not draughtstrip the outer window.

306 Ventilate the space between the double windows to the outside. The gaps around undraughtstripped outer sashes usually provide sufficient ventilation.

307 The risk is avoided by specifying complete double glazing.

308 Where both single and double glazing are used in the same dwelling, ensure that single glazed rooms can be adequately heated and ventilated.

309 Provide ventilation to remove moisture at source (eg kitchens and bathrooms) and adjustable slot ventilators to each room.

310 For single glazed windows, provide drainage channels.

311 For double glazed windows, use metal frames with thermal breaks. In areas of high humidity consider installing metal frames in durable subframes to prevent condensation from the metal frame running directly onto the plaster. [36]

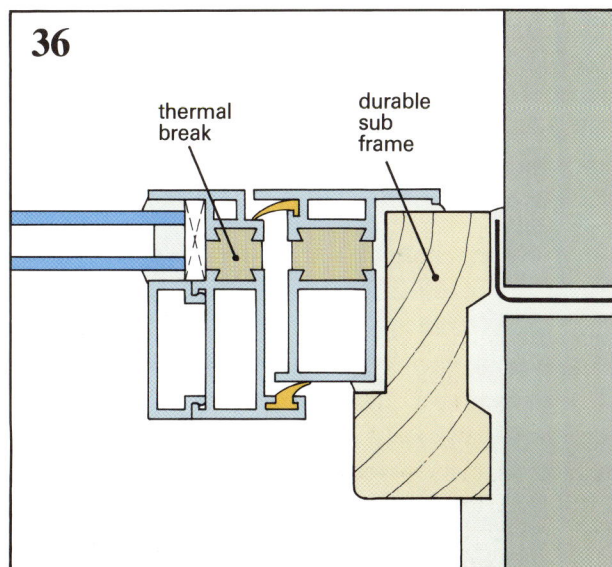

36
thermal break
durable sub frame

4 FLOORS

It has been common practice for floors to be insulated to reduce impact sound and to limit heat loss through floors exposed to the outside air. Current proposals for changes in building regulations include insulation of ground floors for reasons of energy conservation. Thermally insulated floors have been used for a number of years in highly insulated building developments and many systems are available on the market.

The following types of floor are covered:
☐ **Concrete ground floors**
☐ **Timber suspended floors**
☐ **Upper floors**

For **concrete** ground floors, the risks are:
☐ **Loading failures** when the insulation has insufficient strength and rigidity
☐ **Damage** to the insulant and the dpm
☐ **Dampness** problems arising from moisture within the construction
☐ **Cold bridging** at wall junctions and at breaks in the insulation
☐ **Freezing** of water service pipes.

A critical issue for concrete floors is the potential damage to timber boarding or vulnerable floor finishes from moisture rising from an in-situ concrete slab that has not fully dried out.

For **timber** suspended floors and **upper** floors of buildings, the principal risks are:
☐ **Cold bridging** at junctions
☐ **Condensation** within the construction.

CONCRETE GROUND FLOORS

The main forms of concrete ground floor construction are:
☐ **Ground supported** slabs of in-situ concrete
☐ **Suspended** slabs (supported from external walls) of reinforced concrete, beam and block or precast plank.

Suspended slabs may be:
☐ **Unventilated,** or
☐ **Ventilated** (if sufficient depth is available between the slab and the ground beneath).

These floors may be power trowelled, screeded or finished with some form of timber boarding (usually chipboard or plywood).

As most risks for concrete floors are associated with insulation position, the technical issues are illustrated under the following headings:
☐ **Insulation below a screed**
☐ **Insulation below a board**
☐ **Insulation below a slab**

Insulation below a screed

A screeded finish may be used above any form of concrete floor slab, whether ground supported, raft or suspended (in-situ or beam and pot). [37] The potential problems can differ in each case, depending on the type of insulation used, the position of the damp proof membrane and whether the floor is ventilated.

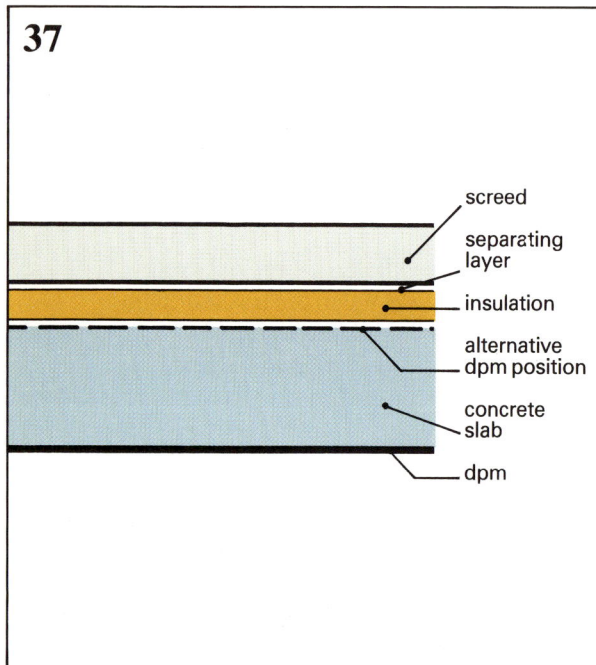

37

screed
separating layer
insulation
alternative dpm position
concrete slab
dpm

Failure under load

When a screed is supported by an insulation board, rather than a totally rigid base such as a concrete slab, great care has to be taken to ensure that the screed is thick enough to counteract the effect of bending when a load is applied. It is also important that screeds are properly compacted above resilient insulation.

401 Use a cement:sand screed of 1:3 to 1:4 mix laid to a minimum thickness of 65mm for domestic construction and 75mm elsewhere.

Lay a separating layer of building paper (to BS 1521, Grade BIF) or polythene sheet (not less than 125 micron or 500 gauge) between the screed and the insulation to prevent the wet screed penetrating the joints between the insulation boards.

402 Choose an insulation board with adequate compressive strength for the intended loading.

403 Ensure that the surface to receive the insulation board is free from mortar or plaster droppings where insulation panels butt together. A roughly tamped concrete surface is not suitable without further treatment. It should be levelled with mortar. A power trowelled surface will be suitable without special treatment. Some precast plank or beam and pot floors will provide a suitable base, if the grout or topping is floated off evenly.

Damage in construction

When screeds are being laid, there is a danger that the insulation board and the membrane above it will be damaged.

404 Use boards across the floor when barrowing and tipping the wet mix and lay light mesh (chicken wire) above the insulant for added protection. [38]

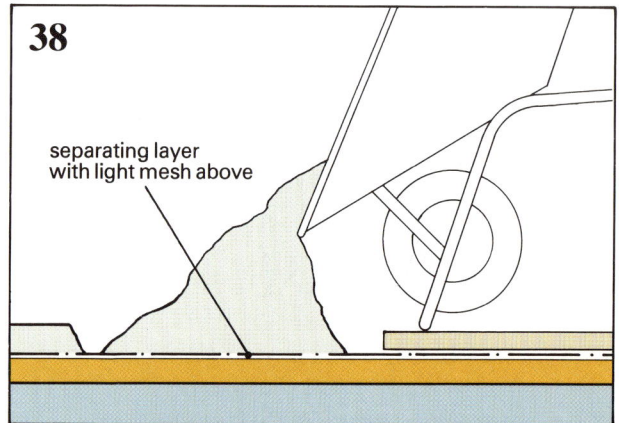

38

separating layer with light mesh above

Damage from construction moisture

Dampness can pass from concrete floor slabs in contact with the ground to the interior and damage vulnerable floor finishes.

405 A damp proof membrane is required. It will reduce the risk of damage if it is positioned above the slab, for example in raft construction.

Dpm beneath the slab
406 Leave the slab to dry for the maximum possible length of time before placing the insulation and laying the screed (not less than 6 months). If this period of time cannot be allowed, then test for moisture content appropriate to the floor finish. Alternatively, upgrade the separating layer to be of dpm standard, ie 1200 gauge polythene sheet. [39]

If a thick slab of lightweight concrete is used, either to reduce the required thickness of the insulation board, or to make its use unnecessary, it is absolutely essential that the construction moisture has fully dried out.

Dpm above the slab
407 Check the compatibility of the insulant with the dpm. [40]

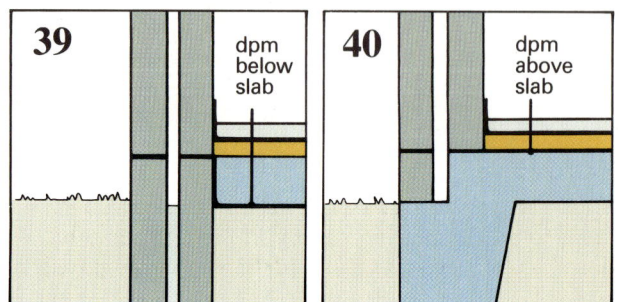

39   dpm below slab

40   dpm above slab

Cold bridges at junctions
Generally, cold bridges will only occur at the junction between the floor and the external wall. A cold bridge also occurs when insulation is omitted, eg at service pipes.

408 Insert a vertical strip of insulation at the perimeter of the screed to provide insulation overlap and increase the length of the cold bridge path. Choose an insulation thickness that can be covered by the wall finish and skirting.

Cavity insulated walls
409 Start the cavity insulation at a point below the lower level of the slab. Where the slab is built into the inner leaf of the wall, use also a block with high insulation value for the inner leaf, commensurate with other requirements of structural stability and sound insulation. [42]

410 Use a suitable insulating block below dpc level when the slab is ground supported.

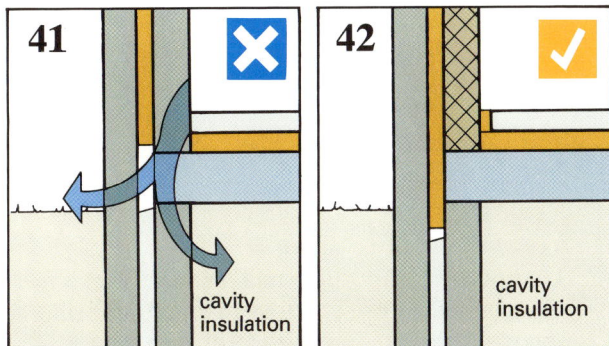

Inner wall leaf insulated
411 No cold bridge exists when the principal insulation value of the wall is provided by the inner leaf, eg in timber frame and clear cavity masonry construction. [43]

Externally insulated walls
412 Insulate the external wall below dpc level and into the ground with a board of high compressive strength and low water absorption, protected with a calcium silicate board or other board unaffected by damp conditions. [44]

Service pipes
413 Ensure that the insulation is cut carefully and fitted tightly around services that pass through the slab. Insulate pipes as they pass through the screed. [46]

Problems associated with services
Services routed within the floor construction can cause problems — puncturing of the dpm or separating membrane, overheating of electric cables etc.

414 Electrical cables may be run in conduit subject to the rules for de-rating if enclosed by insulation. Check whether the size of electrical cables placed within floor insulation, or within the slab immediately below the insulation, needs to be increased to allow for overheating.

45 Alternative position for electrical conduits

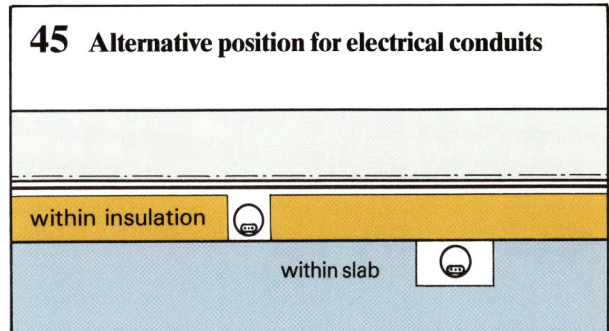

within insulation

within slab

415 Model Water Byelaws do not allow pipes that cannot be withdrawn to be buried within the floor. Do not attempt to run pipes containing water, either potable or for heating, within the floor construction, except the water service pipe. If this pipe rises into the building less than 750mm from the outside face of the external wall, it must be insulated throughout its length. [46]

Use a minimum thickness of 22mm foamed plastics insulation for pipes with an outside diameter up to 42mm. For other types of insulant or sizes of pipe, see Appendix.

This applies to all concrete floors in contact with the ground. For pipes passing through ventilated concrete floors, insulate as for timber suspended floors (see 467).

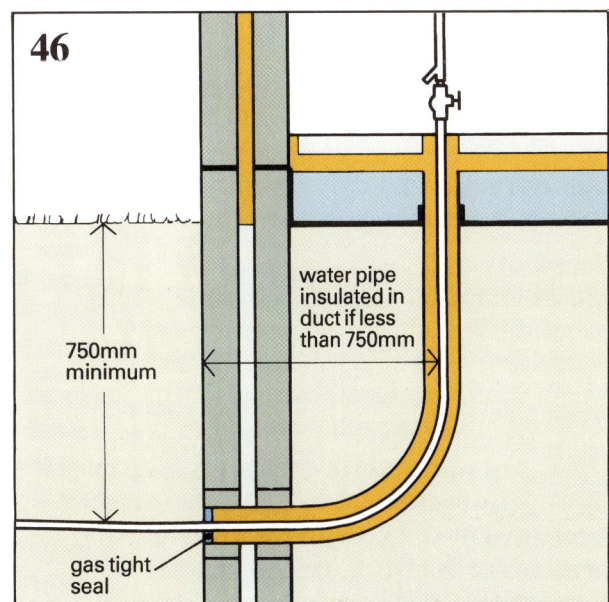

46

water pipe insulated in duct if less than 750mm

750mm minimum

gas tight seal

Insulation below a board

Systems with insulation beneath chipboard or plywood panels have been used for many years as 'floating floors' to control impact sound in flats. When used for thermal insulation purposes, the insulant does not need to be resilient, indeed, there are advantages in it being as rigid as possible.

The main technical issue is how to prevent moisture weakening the board finish, whether from within the construction or from spillages.

The insulated floor finish can be constructed with:
☐ **Composite panels** using chipboard and a rigid insulant [47]
☐ **Loose laid systems** with the chipboard or plywood boards and the rigid insulant installed separately [48]
☐ **Timber battens** supporting boards with resilient insulant between the battens. [49]

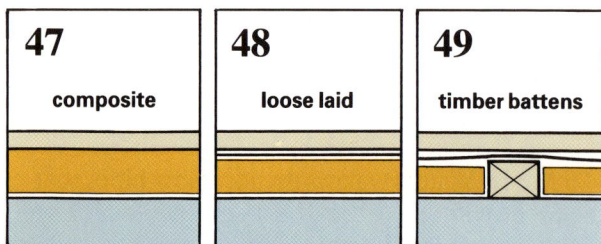

47 composite

48 loose laid

49 timber battens

Uneven floor surface
An uneven floor surface may result from point loads or regular traffic, if the floor boarding is not adequately supported.

416 Ensure that the surface of the sub-floor is flat as for screeded floors (see 404).

417 Fit tongued and grooved chipboard panels tightly together and glue the joints using a PVA or mastic adhesive and temporary wedges at the perimeter.

418 Lightly sand and sweep chipboard floors to make the surface suitable for thin flooring such as vinyl. Do not wash or scrub with water.

419 Provide a gap at all edges of timber flooring to allow for moisture expansion. Allow 10mm, or 2mm per metre run of floor whichever is the greater at all abutments between walls and timber boards. This is particularly important for chipboard floors.

Composite and loose laid systems
420 If the insulant supports the boarding, select a type which has sufficient compressive strength to avoid depressions or indentations under load, whether the insulation is separate from the finish or combined with it in a composite panel.

421 Screw cut edges of boarding at door openings to preservative treated timber support battens. [50] Ensure that these timbers are on a firm and level base, but not fixed to the slab, to allow for movement in the floor panels. Use additional support battens where extra floor loading is anticipated, eg beneath kitchen fittings and equipment, but not at the perimeter of the floor.

Boarding on timber battens
422 There is no compressive strength requirement for the insulant between battened floors. To prevent an uneven surface, do not attempt to fix flooring to the battens through resilient insulation material. [51]

50 ✓

51 ✗

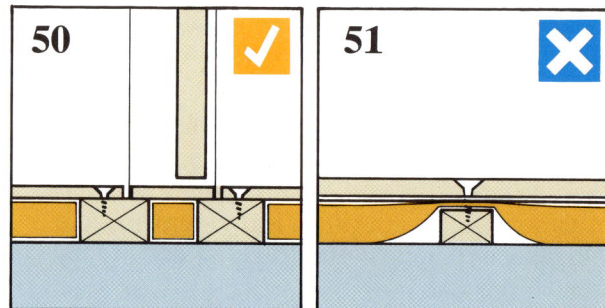

Damage from construction moisture
Timber boarded floors, particularly those using chipboard, are extremely vulnerable to damage from construction moisture and certain insulation systems are acceptable only above concrete floors of dry precast construction.

Dpm beneath an in-situ slab
423 Do not use composite panels or timber batten systems where the dpm is below an in-situ slab that has not dried out for at least 6 months, or test for acceptable moisture content. [53]

424 If the slab is not fully dry, use a loose laid system, but lay a moisture resisting layer of dpm standard (1200 gauge polythene) between the rigid plastics insulation and the timber boarding, lap and tape the joints and turn up the membrane 100mm behind the skirting. [52]

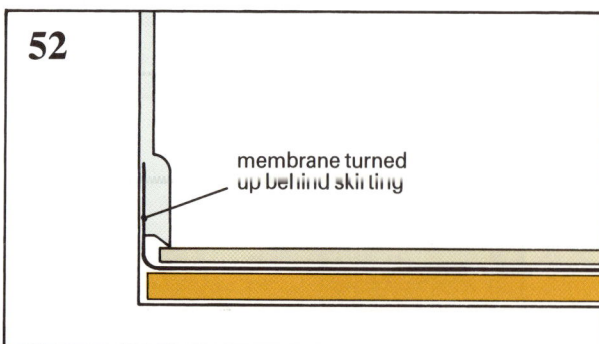

52 membrane turned up behind skirting

Dpm above an in-situ slab
425 Use composite or loose laid flooring systems in this circumstance, but check the compatibility of the insulant with the dpm.

Precast units (dry construction)
426 Any timber flooring system can be used above precast concrete units that have a limited amount of 'wet' topping (grout or concrete).

Composite panels

427 Composite panels may be used above any type of concrete floor. However, where the concrete structure has not fully dried out, a dpm is required above the slab.

Loose laid systems

428 Loose laid timber boarding systems which have glued joints and tightly butted closed cell rigid plastics insulation boards require no moisture resisting membrane to protect the timber if the in-situ concrete slab has fully dried out, or if the structure below is precast concrete (dry) construction.

429 If the slab has not fully dried out, either use a moisture resisting membrane of 500 gauge polythene above the insulation (in addition to a dpm below the slab) or alternatively, locate the dpm above the slab.

Boarding on timber battens

430 Always use a moisture resisting membrane of 500 gauge polythene sheet between the boarding and the timber support battens above all in-situ slabs, irrespective of dpm position. Ensure that the timber battens are preservative treated by pressure impregnation.

431 A moisture resisting membrane is not required beneath the timber boarding when it is above a ventilated (dry) precast floor, because the amount of construction moisture is small and, if condensation occurs on the top of the flooring units, it is unlikely to be harmful. Without a membrane, water spillage will also drain away more easily.

> **Condensation within the construction**
> Condensation may form on the top surface of the concrete slab.

432 The risk is small, provided moisture resisting membranes are installed to protect the timber boarding. A ventilated sub-floor will reduce the risk further. The advice given for resisting moisture damage to timber flooring will be adequate to avoid condensation within the floor construction.

> **Cold bridges at junctions**
> As the insulation is above the slab, cold bridges are possible in the same positions as when the insulation is below a screed. The possibilities for providing insulation overlap by inserting a vertical strip of insulation do not exist because the timber boarding is not as thick as the screed.

433 Follow the guidance given in paragraphs 409 to 413.

> **Long term damage from water spillage**
> Water spillage from household fittings and leaking services is potentially much more damaging for a timber floor than for a screeded floor, particularly if the floor boarding is chipboard.
>
> Measures taken to prevent the floor boarding being damaged by construction moisture will cause spilt water to be contained on or within the boarding itself.
>
> Action can usually be taken to limit the damage from small scale spillage. If substantial quantities of water reach the floor, the boarding will almost certainly need to be replaced.

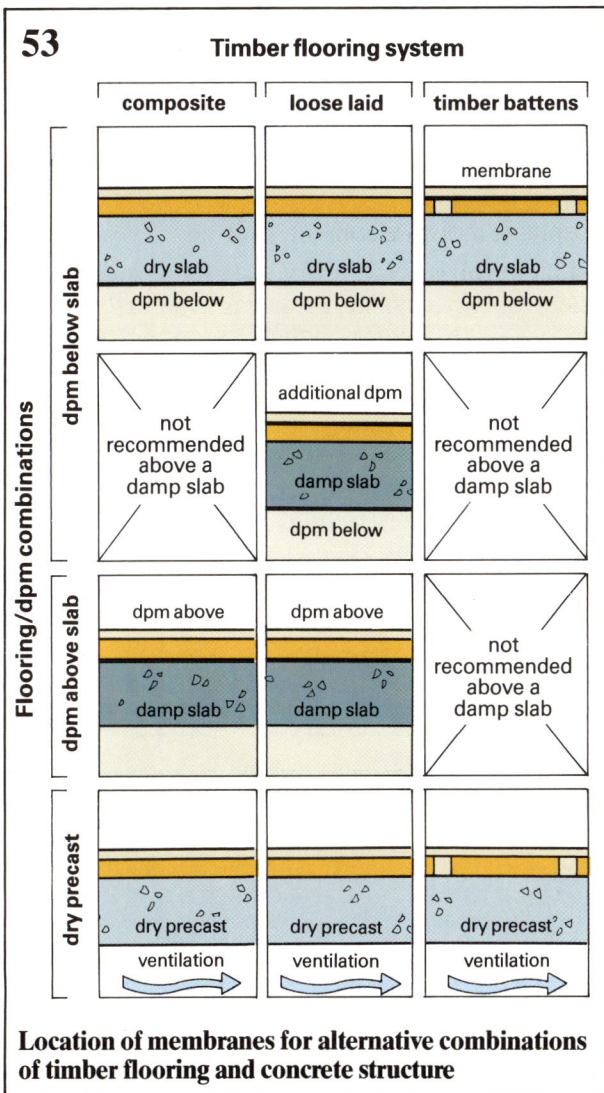

434 Limit damage to the flooring panels, especially in *kitchens* and *bathrooms,* by using chipboard flooring to BS 5669, Type II/III, and tested so as to swell by no more than 8% of the original thickness according to the V313 cyclic test.

435 The floor boarding can be protected from minor spillage by sealing the surface with a polyurethane sealer. Greater protection can be achieved by using a fully impermeable floor finish such as vinyl sheet with welded joints and skirting.

53 Timber flooring system

	composite	loose laid	timber battens
dpm below slab	dry slab / dpm below	dry slab / dpm below	membrane / dry slab / dpm below
	not recommended above a damp slab	additional dpm / damp slab / dpm below	not recommended above a damp slab
dpm above slab	dpm above / damp slab	dpm above / damp slab	not recommended above a damp slab
dry precast	dry precast / ventilation	dry precast / ventilation	dry precast / ventilation

Location of membranes for alternative combinations of timber flooring and concrete structure

Insulation below a slab

Insulation may be positioned below both ground supported slabs and reinforced concrete suspended slabs supported by a masonry external wall. [54, 55]

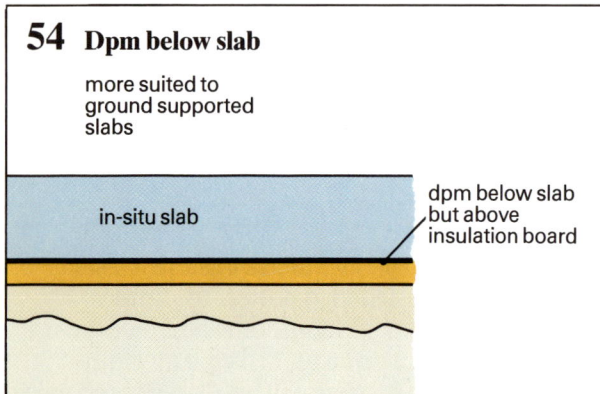

54 Dpm below slab

more suited to ground supported slabs

in-situ slab

dpm below slab but above insulation board

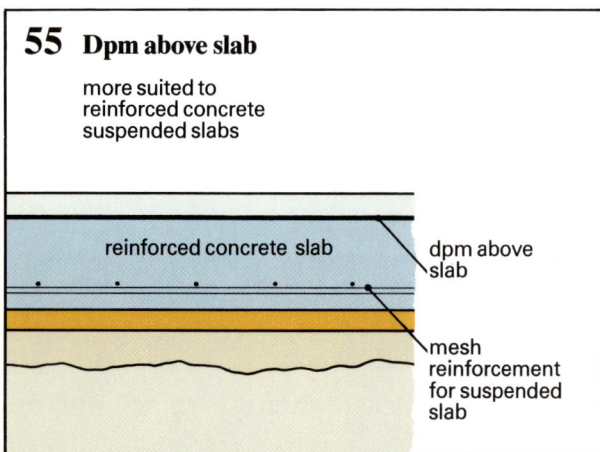

55 Dpm above slab

more suited to reinforced concrete suspended slabs

reinforced concrete slab

dpm above slab

mesh reinforcement for suspended slab

Failure due to floor loading

As ground supported slabs are cast directly onto the insulation, deformation of the insulation could lead to initial subsidence of the floor, unexpected stresses in the floor slab and a reduction in the thermal performance of the floor.

---

436 Use an insulant with low water absorption and high resistance to ground contaminants so that its thermal properties are maintained over the life of the building.

Ground supported slabs

437 Choose an insulant which is of sufficient compressive strength to support the required floor loading. Ensure that the hardcore is well consolidated and made flat with sand blinding.

Damage during construction

Care is needed to prevent the dpm and the insulation materials being displaced or damaged, not only across the floor itself, but also at the junction with the external wall.

---

438 Use boards for walking and barrowing across the dpm and insulation when concreting.

439 Take extra care before the concrete is poured because, when sharp objects fall, they can penetrate both the dpm and the insulation.

440 Ensure that the insulation boards fit tightly together and are weighed down as necessary before and after laying the dpm.

Ground supported slabs

441 When pouring, tamping and power trowelling, protect the insulation and the dpm, for example with temporary timber battens, where they turn up vertically to meet the wall dpc. [56, 57]

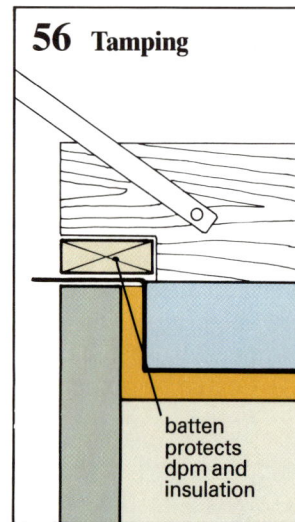

56 Tamping

batten protects dpm and insulation

57 Power trowelling

insulation turn-up difficult

Reinforced concrete slabs

442 Take care not to puncture the dpm when placing the reinforcement.

Cold bridges at junctions

The greatest risk of condensation occurs at the junction of the floor and the external wall, and also at loadbearing internal walls.

Inner wall leaf insulated

443 Turn the insulation up vertically at the edge of ground supported slabs. [58] A cold bridge through suspended slabs cannot be avoided if the wall is insulated in this way. [59]

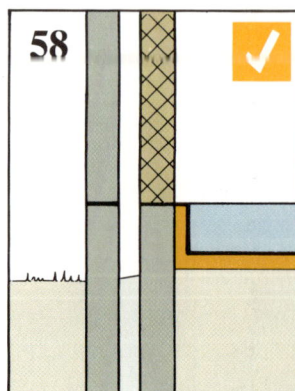

58 ✓

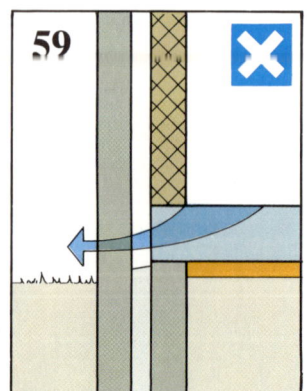

59 ✗

444 For suspended slabs, where the floor insulation cannot be turned up on the face of the wall, cavity insulation is necessary to avoid the cold bridge. [60]

Cavity and externally insulated walls

445 Always start the cavity insulation below the bottom of the floor slab. Use a low density block for the inner leaf of the wall, particularly below dpc (see 410). **[60]**

446 Insulate the external wall below dpc level (see 412). In the case of suspended slabs, further benefit can be obtained by continuing the insulation board vertically downwards on the inside face of the external wall. **[61]**

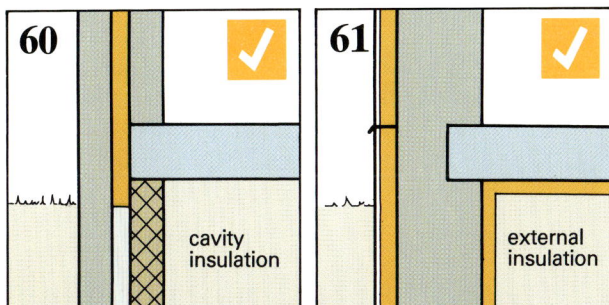

60
cavity insulation

61
external insulation

Loadbearing internal walls

447 For ground supported slabs, vertical edge insulation reduces the risk of cold bridging. For extra protection, place insulation against each face of the wall below slab level, or use a low density block below dpc. **[62]**

448 Where foundation walls support a reinforced concrete slab, place insulation on each face of the wall to lengthen the cold bridge path. **[63]**

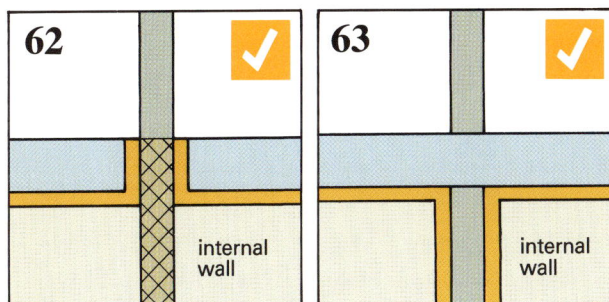

62
internal wall

63
internal wall

Stepped separating walls

449 Where slabs are ground supported, face only one side of the separating wall with insulation. **[64]** If the slabs are built into the wall, face both sides with insulation. **[65]**

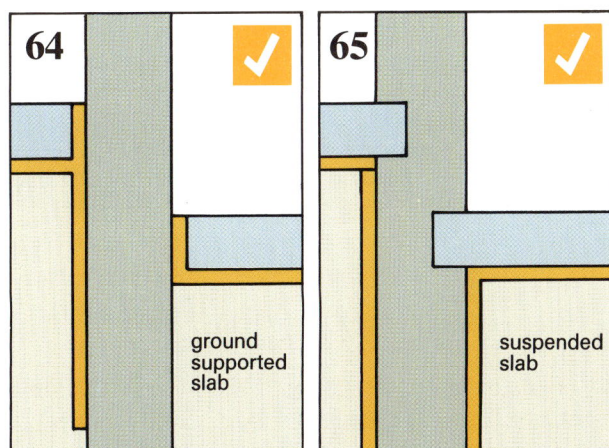

64
ground supported slab

65
suspended slab

Damage from construction moisture and rising damp
Damage can be caused by dampness from the ground and vapour from inside the building. When the slab is cast in-situ, construction moisture can damage floor finishes.

450 With the insulation below the floor slab, resistance to dampness from the ground and vapour control from inside the building can be provided by a single membrane. Place the dpm above an insulation board that is resistant to moisture and grond contaminants.

451 Use 1200 gauge polythene sheet welted and taped at joints and link it with the wall dpc. For ground supported slabs, the polythene will tend to keep the vertical strip of insulation in place.

452 Do not use floor finishes that are susceptible to moisture, unless the slab has dried for at least 6 months. Alternatively, lay the finish on a separate dpm.

Ground supported slabs

453 Keep the dpm to the inside of the vertical "edge-of-slab" insulation. This will help to keep the short strip of insulation in position whilst concreting. **[66]**

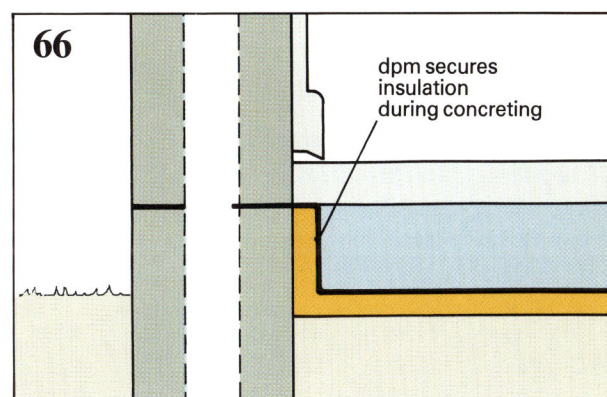

66
dpm secures insulation during concreting

Suspended slabs

454 Ensure a firm base for the dpm and insulation to avoid the membrane being torn as it meets the external wall. Turn up the membrane within the cavity to link with the wall dpc. **[67]**

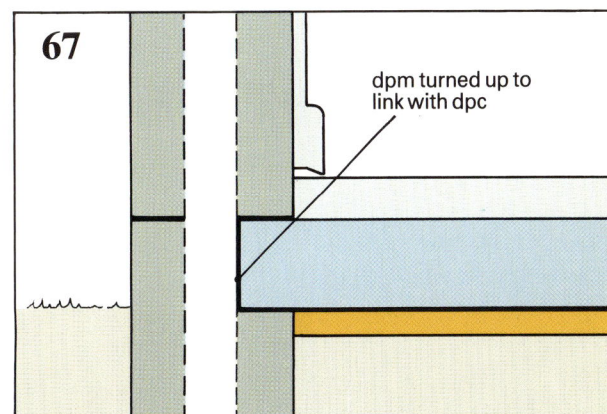

67
dpm turned up to link with dpc

TIMBER SUSPENDED FLOORS

Insulation between the joists

For timber floors insulated between the joists, the method of insulation is normally:
- [ ] Quilt supported in plastics mesh [68], or
- [ ] Rigid boards supported on battens, corrosion resistant nails or clips. [69]

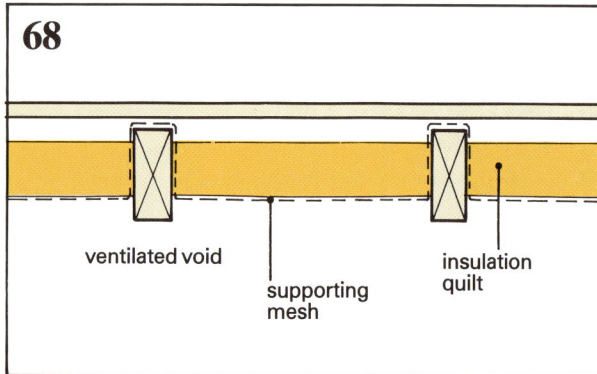

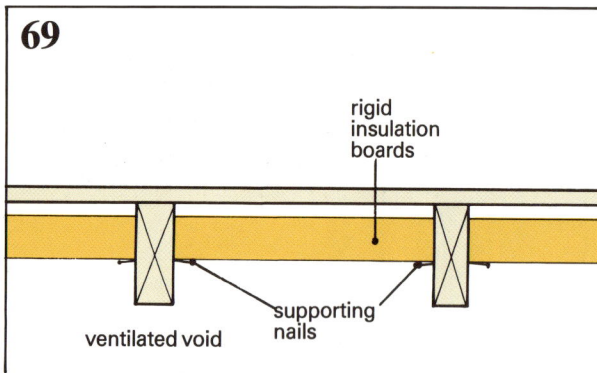

68

ventilated void
supporting mesh
insulation quilt

69

rigid insulation boards
ventilated void
supporting nails

Uneven floor surface
An uneven floor surface can occur if the flooring cannot be nailed down to a firm base.

455 Do not attempt to fix flooring through quilt which has been draped over the floor joists, as uneven compression can lead to an unsatisfactory finish and a squeaky floor. [70]

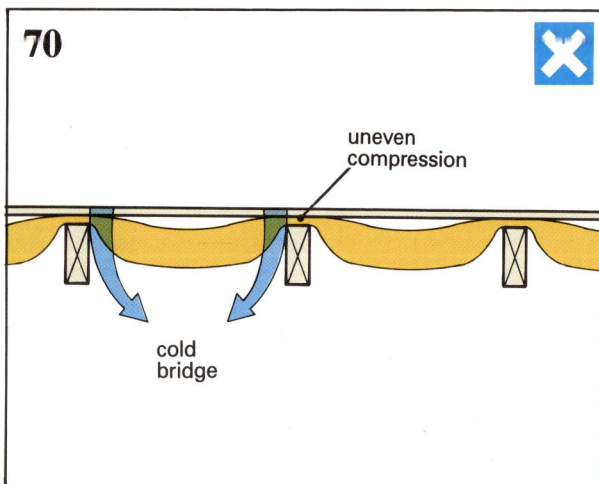

70

uneven compression
cold bridge

Cold bridges through the floor and at junctions
There will be a potential cold bridge where the full insulation value of the floor is not maintained because the thickness of the insulation is reduced or air leakage occurs through the construction.

456 Maintain insulation continuity between the floor and the wall by filling any space between joists and the wall with insulation.

457 For cavity insulated and externally insulated walls, use blockwork with the highest practicable insulation value. The greatest continuity is maintained when the inner leaf and/or lining provides the major insulation contribution. [73, 74]

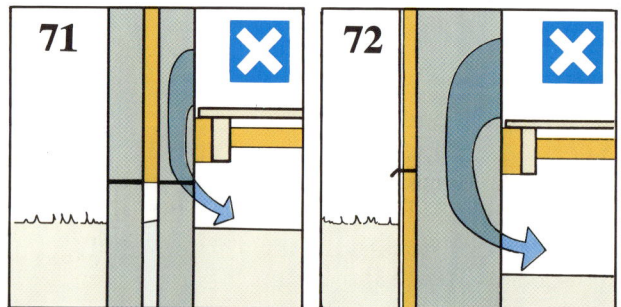

71

72

73

74

458 To prevent air leakage between the floor and the wall, seal the gap between the floor and the wall with tape or a sealant.

459 Ensure that no structural member of high thermal conductivity, such as a steel beam, is immediately beneath the floor finish. [75, 76]

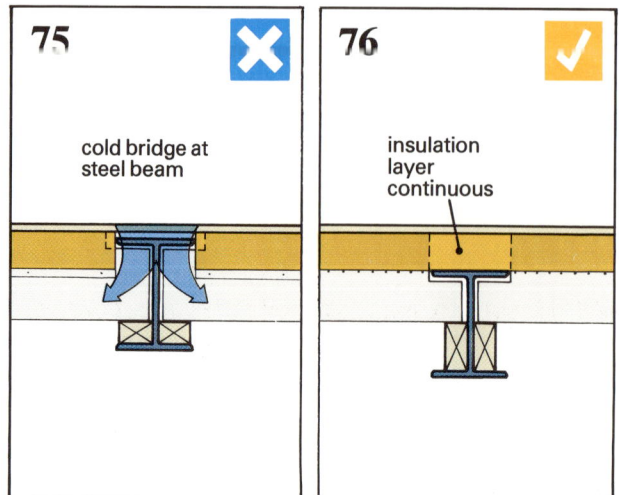

75

cold bridge at steel beam

76

insulation layer continuous

Quilt insulation
460 Do not drape quilt insulation over timber joists as its thickness will be reduced at the joists.

461 If a paper faced quilt is used, lay with the paper face to the underside, to prevent water spillage affecting timber flooring.

462 Staple plastics mesh support to the sides of the joists so that the insulation quilt can be laid full thickness between the joists. **[77]** Alternatively, fix a vapour permeable board, such as fibreboard, towards the bottom of the joists to support the insulation and also reduce air movement through it.

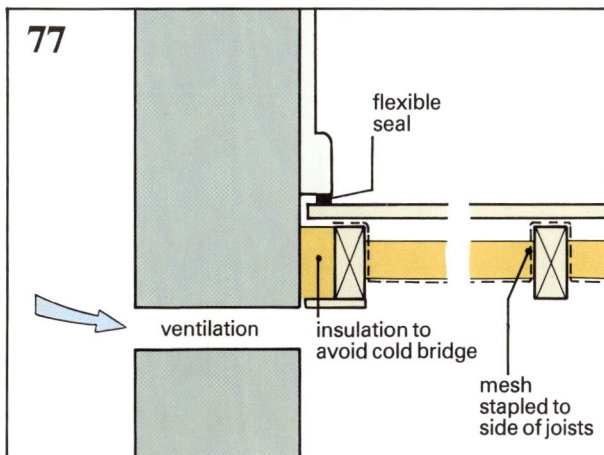

Rigid board insulation
463 If rigid insulation boards are used, ensure they fit tightly between the joists to avoid air leakage through the floor. **[78]**

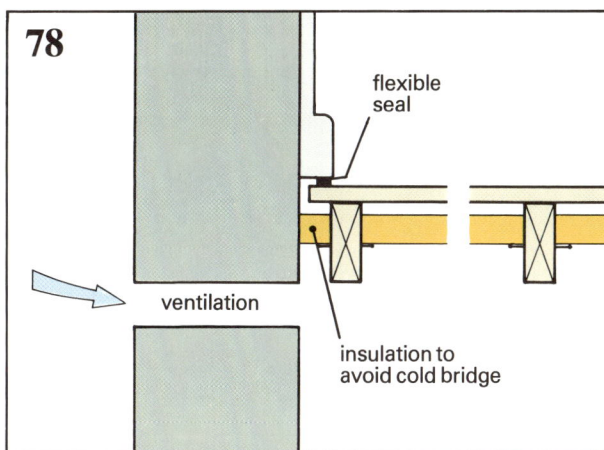

Condensation within the construction
With suspended timber floors, small amounts of condensation may form. They can be ventilated away.

464 It is not necessary to introduce a vapour barrier into the construction. Ensure that the sub-floor space is cross ventilated through openings in the wall not less than either 1500mm² per metre run of external wall, or 500mm² per square metre of floor area, whichever gives the larger opening area. (BS 5250)

Long term damage from water spillage
For suspended timber floors, the potential damage from water spillage affects not only the floor boarding, but also the timber structure. Without a vapour barrier, water will soak through the floor and gradually ventilate away.

465 When chipboard flooring is to be used in rooms at greatest risk such as kitchens and bathrooms, use a moisture resistant type (see 434) and consider protecting the floor with a polyurethane sealer or welded vinyl flooring (see 435).

466 Allow an expansion gap of 10mm, or 2mm per metre run of floor, whichever is the greater, at the perimeter of chipboard flooring.

Problems associated with services
Water services beneath the floor are at risk from freezing if not insulated, and electrical cables at risk from overheating if embedded in insulation.

467 Water service pipes that pass through a ventilated space must be insulated, irrespective of their distance from the external wall. **[79]** Use foamed plastics insulation at least 27mm thick for pipes up to 42mm outside diameter. For other insulation materials or pipe sizes, see Appendix.

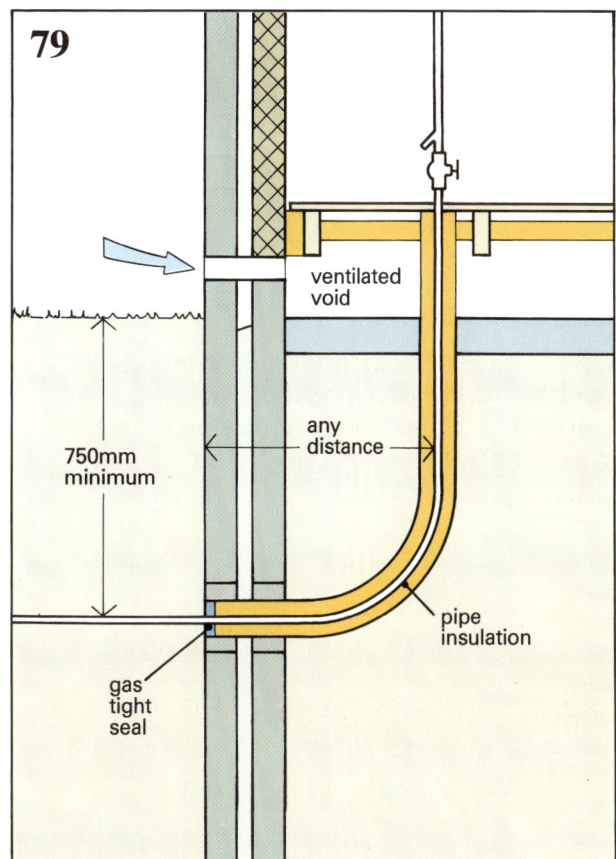

468 For electrical cables serving cookers and electric shower units, follow the guidance in the Appendix.

UPPER FLOORS

Upper floors of buildings are insulated against heat loss only when their soffit is exposed to the outside air or to an unheated or ventilated space.

The principal technical risk is condensation, whether surface condensation due to cold bridges at junctions between a floor and the external wall, or interstitial condensation within a floor with an exposed soffit.

Intermediate floors

Intermediate floors present potential problems when they are built into the external wall, or when they extend through it to form balconies or other features.

Cold bridges at junctions

When a concrete intermediate floor is built into a masonry external wall, the beam width is greater than the inner leaf and must project either into the wall cavity or into the room. If the beam projects too far into a filled cavity wall, there may be insufficient insulation remaining to avoid a cold bridge.

If the floor projects to the face of the wall or beyond it to form a balcony, the wall insulation is inevitably interrupted and the floor must be insulated to reduce the risk of condensation.

Floors with a concrete beam
469 Project the concrete beam into the room rather than the wall cavity, so as to maintain the full thickness of thermal insulation. [80, 81]

470 If beams project into the cavity, maintain a minimum of 25mm insulation in the cavity. [82]

471 Use cavity or external insulation in preference to internal insulation, unless both floor and ceiling are to be insulated. [83]

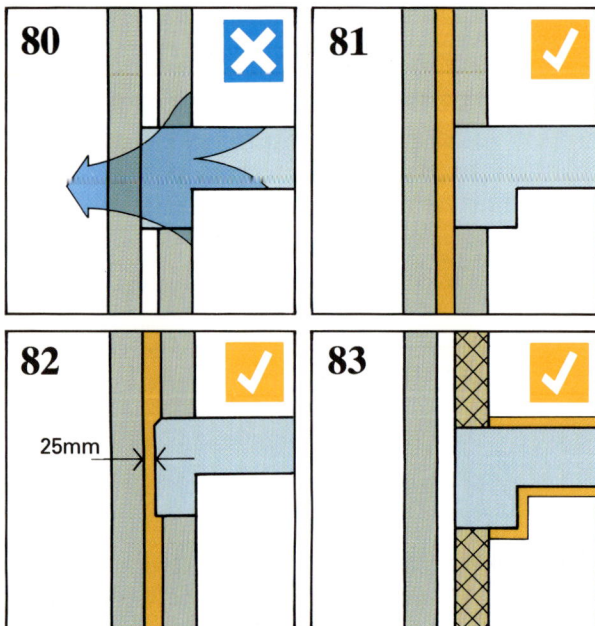

Floors projecting through the wall
472 Return ceiling insulation, equivalent to 25mm of expanded polystyrene at least 2 metres into the room from the external wall and insulate the upper surface of the floor slab inside the building. [84, 85]

473 If cavity insulation is used, choose a low density block for the inner leaf. [85]

474 Insulation of the inner leaf or lining provides the greatest continuity in avoiding a cold bridge.

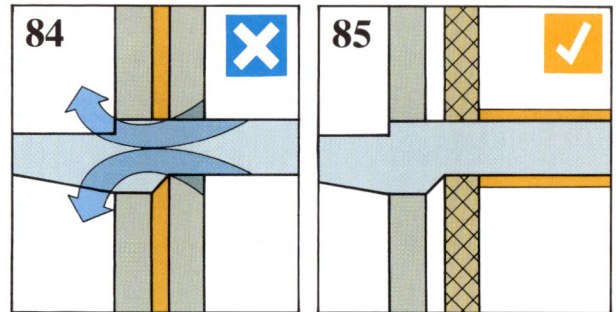

All concrete floor to wall junctions
475 Where cavity insulation is interrupted or cavities extend over several storeys, follow published guidance on:
- Cavity trays and weepholes
- Damp proofing and concrete beams
- Allowance for movement in masonry
- Cavity barriers
- Support for the outer leaf at intermediate floor junctions. [86]

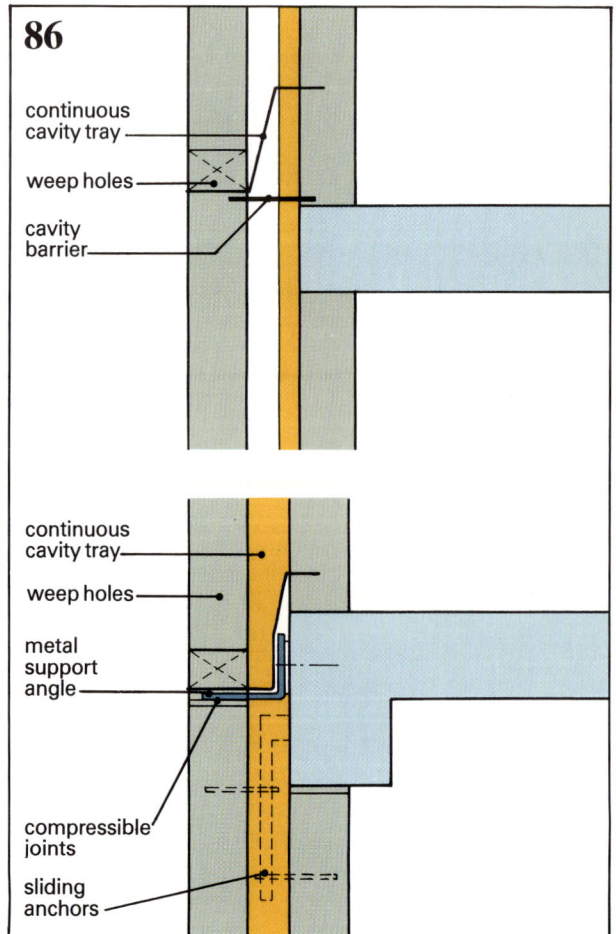

continuous cavity tray

weep holes

cavity barrier

continuous cavity tray

weep holes

metal support angle

compressible joints

sliding anchors

Exposed soffit floors

Exposed soffit floors are not affected by loading and damp proofing considerations, but they are susceptible to risks from cold bridging, interstitial condensation and damage from water spillage.

Cold bridges at junctions
Where exposed soffit floors join external walls, there is likely to be a cold bridge. It is more difficult to avoid when floors meet a concrete edge beam.

476 Choose cavity or internal wall insulation in preference to external.

Concrete floors
477 Avoiding cold bridges at concrete floors can be difficult and every effort should be made to ensure that insulation is continuous at wall/floor junctions. [89, 90]

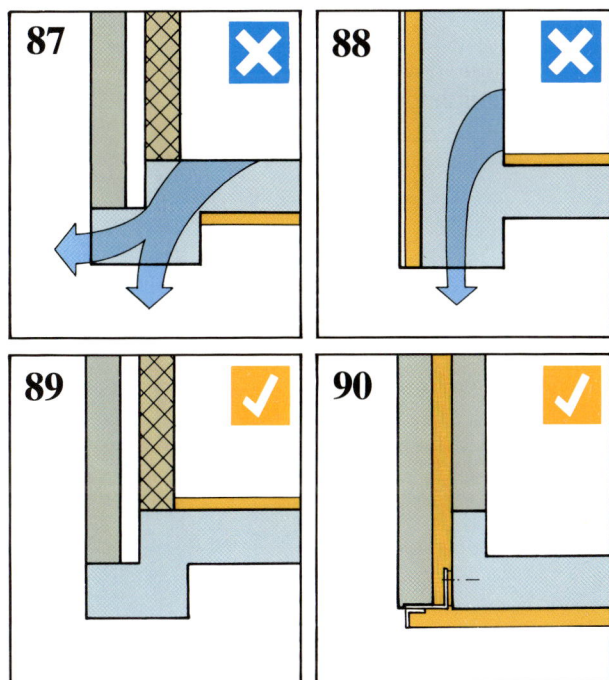

Timber floors
478 Insulate all gaps adjacent to the wall and use either a block with a high insulation value for the inner leaf, or internal insulation. [91, 92]

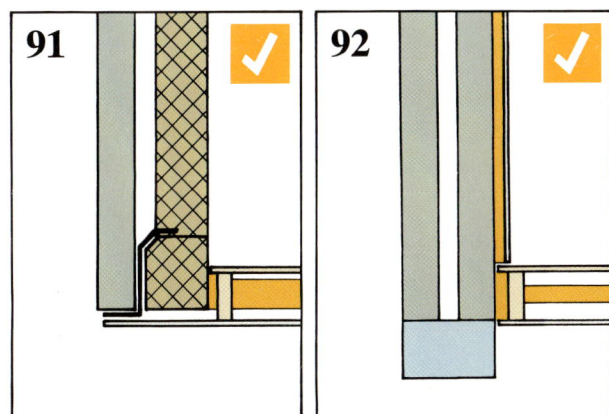

Condensation within the construction
When timber floors are laid directly on metal or concrete joists, condensation on the top of the joists may cause collapse, as a cold bridge is formed through the insulation. Interstitial condensation is unlikely to be a problem in concrete floors.

Concrete floors
479 Ensure that the soffit lining is a material with a low vapour resistance. If a high vapour resistance external layer is unavoidable, provide a 50mm ventilation space behind it, with openings in opposite edges of the soffit, equivalent to a continuous gap of 25mm. [93]

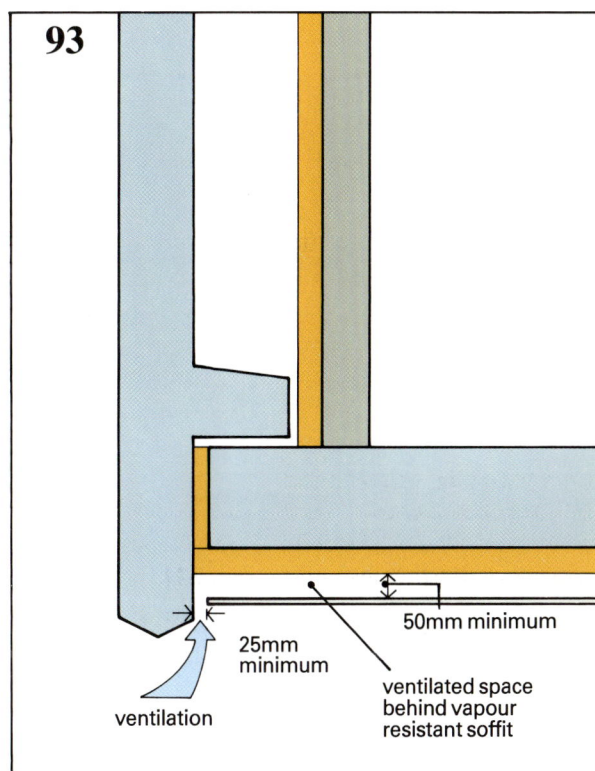

50mm minimum

25mm minimum

ventilation

ventilated space behind vapour resistant soffit

Timber floors
480 Do not use a vapour check within the construction.

481 Ensure that materials which support the insulation or provide the soffit lining have a low vapour resistance.

Long term damage from water spillage
The risk of damage from water spillage is less with timber exposed floors as there is no vapour check to prevent spilt water draining through.

482 Take precautions with chipboard flooring as outlined in 434 and 435.

Timber floors
483 Use insulation materials which allow spilt water to drain freely through the floor and to the outside.

Supplementary data

INSULATION THICKNESS FOR WATER SUPPLY PIPES

Insulation thickness should be chosen to suit *indoor* and *outdoor* standards as follows:

Indoor standard
- Pipes in ducts within solid concrete ground floors
- Pipes within the insulated enclosure but close to cold spots.

Outdoor standard
- Pipes passing through ventilated floors
- Pipes routed outside the insulated enclosure.

Table 7 Minimum thickness of pipe insulation (data taken from BS 6700: 1987)

| Nominal outside diameter of pipe [mm] | Thermal conductivity of insulating materials not exceeding | | | | | | | |
| | 0.035 W/mK | | 0.04 W/mK | | 0.055 W/mK | | 0.07 W/mK | |
	Indoor [mm]	Outdoor [mm]	Indoor [mm]	Outdoor [mm]	Indoor [mm]	Outdoor [mm]	Indoor [mm]	Outdoor [mm]
Up to 15	22	27	32	38	50	63	89	100
Over 15 up to 22	22	27	32	38	50	63	75	100
Over 22 up to 42	22	27	32	38	50	63	75	89
Over 42 up to 54	16	19	25	32	44	50	63	75
Over 54 up to 76.1	13	16	25	25	32	44	50	63
Over 76.1 and flat surfaces	13	16	19	25	25	32	38	50

Typical insulating materials:
- Polyurethane foam or foamed or expanded plastics, including rigid and flexible preformed pipe insulation of these materials
- Cork
- Exfoliated vermiculite (loose fill)
- Mineral wool

SIZES FOR CABLES ENCLOSED WITHIN INSULATION

Where electrical cables are covered by insulation on one side (0.75 derating factor) and protected by cartridge fuses, the following circuits should have their cable sizes increased to $6/2.5\text{mm}^2$

- 30 amp cooker control unit.
- 30 amp radial circuit supplying either a 6kW shower or socket outlets.

Other circuits can normally accept being derated to 0.75 without exceeding their current carrying capacity. To comply with the IEE Wiring Regulations, the designer must provide detailed drawings and design calculations.

Sources of information

British Standards Institution

BS476 *Fire tests on building materials and structures.* Part 6: 1968 and 1981 *Method of test for fire propagation for products.* Part 7: 1971 and 1987 *Method for classification of the surface spread of flame of products.* Part 8: 1972 *Tests methods and criteria for the fire resistance of elements of building construction.* Part 20: 1987 *Method for determination of fire resistance of elements of construction (general principles).*

BS 747: 1977 *Specification for roofing felts.*

BS 1521: 1972 *Specification for waterproof building papers.*

BS 3921: 1985 *Specification for clay bricks.*

BS 4016: 1972 *Specification for building papers (breather type).*

BS 5250: 1988 *Code of basic data for the design of buildings: The control of condensation in dwellings.*

BS 5618: 1985 *Code of practice for thermal insulation of cavity walls (with masonry or concrete inner and outer leaves) by filling with urea-formaldehyde (UF) foam systems.*

BS 5628 *Code of practice for use of masonry.* Part 3: 1985 *Materials and components, design and workmanship.*

BS 5669: 1979 *Specification for wood chipboard and methods of test for particle board.*

BS 6232 *Thermal insulation of cavity walls by filling with blown man-made mineral fibre.* Part 1: 1982 *Specifications for the perfomance of installation systems.*

BS 6676 *Thermal insulation of cavity walls using man-made mineral fibre batts (slabs).* Part 2: 1986 *Code of practice for installation of batts (slabs) filling the cavity.*

BS 6700: 1987 *Specification for design, installation, testing and maintenance of services supplying water for domestic use within buildings and their curtilages.*

BS 8208: *Guide to assessment of suitability of external cavity walls for filling with thermal insulants.* Part 1: 1985 *Existing traditional cavity construction.*

BSI Draft for Development DD93: 1984 *Methods for assessing exposure to wind driven rain.*

Building Research Establishment

BRE Defect Action Sheet 109 *Hot and cold water systems — protection against frost.*

BRE Digest 236 *Cavity insulation*

BRE Digest 277 *Built-in cavity wall insulation for housing.*

Glass and Glazing Federation

Glazing techniques for insulating glass units.

London Brick Company

Climate and brickwork: *Constructional notes,* October 1988.

BBA, BEC, BRE, NHBC

Cavity insulation of masonry walls — Dampness risks and how to minimise them.

Institution of Electrical Engineers

Regulations of electrical installations, 15th edition, 1981.

INDEX

Printed in the UK for HMSO Dd.8339414, 12/91, C50, 38938